Henry Adams wrote:

"You have gone so far beyond me, both in horizon and in study, that I feel our situations reversed. You are the professor; and I am the student."

Thus Henry Adams expressed tribute to his former student, Henry Osborn Taylor. Yet at the time Taylor was the student there was no suggestion that he would one day take up history as his profession. After graduating from Harvard in 1878 he studied law, receiving his degree from Columbia University in 1881. However, law was not his calling, and he took up the study of Western culture instead.

Born in New York City on December 5, 1856, Taylor is of the generation of outstanding American historians whose company includes Lynn Thorndike, James Harvey Robinson, and Preserved Smith. He died in New York City on April 13, 1941.

In addition to *Thought and Expression in the Sixteenth Century,* of which *Erasmus and Luther* is Book 2, Taylor's works include *Ancient Ideals, A Study of the Intellectual and Spiritual Growth from Early Times to the Establishment of Christianity* (2 vols., 2nd ed. 1913), *Freedom of the Mind in History* (2nd ed. 1924), and *A Historian's Creed* (1939). His most important work is *The Medieval Mind* (2 vols., 5th ed. 1938).

The five books of *Thought and Expression in the Sixteenth Century,* all available in Collier paperbacks, are:

The Humanism of Italy (AS437)

Erasmus and Luther (AS438)

The French Mind (AS439)

The English Mind (AS440)

Philosophy and Science in the Sixteenth Century (AS441)

HENRY OSBORN TAYLOR

ERASMUS

AND LUTHER

BOOK 2 OF *Thought and Expression in the Sixteenth Century*

COLLIER BOOKS

NEW YORK, N.Y.

This Collier Books edition is published by arrangement with
The President and Fellows of Harvard College

Collier Books is a division of The Crowell-Collier Publishing
Company

First Collier Books Edition 1962

TO

J. I. T.

About the Author

HENRY OSBORN TAYLOR belongs to the outstanding generation of American historians that includes Lynn Thorndike, James Harvey Robinson, and Preserved Smith. He was born December 5, 1856, in New York City, and died there on April 13, 1941. Taylor was graduated from Harvard in 1878 and received a degree in law from Columbia University in 1881. Law was not his calling, however, and he soon began to devote himself to the study of Western culture.

Thought and Expression in the Sixteenth Century (2 vols., 1920) and *The Medieval Mind* (2 vols., 5th ed. 1938) are classics in the historiography of ideas in America.

Other books by Taylor include his first work, *Ancient Ideals, a Study of the Intellectual and Spiritual Growth from Early Times to the Establishment of Christianity* (2 vols., 2nd ed. 1913), *Freedom of the Mind in History* (2nd ed. 1924), and *A Historian's Creed* (1939).

Thought and Expression in the Sixteenth Century is now published by Collier Books in five volumes, each of which may be read independently: *The Humanism of Italy, Erasmus and Luther, The French Mind, The English Mind,* and *Philosophy and Science in the Renaissance* are the titles of the separate volumes in this new edition.

Note

Many studies of Luther and Erasmus have appeared since Taylor wrote *Erasmus and Luther*, the second part of *Thought and Expression in the Sixteenth Century*, in 1920. Yet as a consequence of Taylor's careful and sensitive scholarship, *Erasmus and Luther* remains a worthy guide to the lives and careers of these two central figures of the northern Renaissance.

In his examination of the humanist's enormous influence on education and intellect, Taylor says of Erasmus, "His life was an education for himself and his age." Through tract and religious writing, through epoch-making editions and translations, through imaginative and symbolic satire, Erasmus used scholarship in a spirit of temperance and irony in order to produce a better understanding of Christianity.

Turning to Luther, Taylor explains much that is obscure in the reformer's thought. He discusses the various influences upon Luther in a way that makes clear to the reader Luther's crucial role in the spiritual and political revolution that we have come to know as the Reformation.

Nowhere else does Taylor combine the historical and the thematic approach with the same strength of coherence as in *Erasmus and Luther*. The breadth of information and intelligence of assessment are such that any reader will find his perspective on the Renaissance in Europe deepened and enlarged.

Contents

Preface

My purpose is to give an intellectual survey of the sixteenth century. I would set forth the human susceptibilities and faculties of this alluring time, it takes, opinions and appreciations, as they expressed themselves in scholarship and literature, in philosophy and science, and in religious reform. Italian painting is presented briefly as the supreme self-expression of the Italians.

The more typical intellectual interests of the fifteenth century also are discussed for their own sake, while those of the previous time are treated as introductory. I have tried to show the vital continuity between the prior mediaeval development and the period before us.

The mind must fetch a far compass if it would see the sixteenth century truly. Every stage in the life and thought of Europe represents a passing phase, which is endowed with faculties not begotten of itself, and brings forth much that is not exclusively its own. For good or ill, for patent progress, or apparent retrogression, its capacities, idiosyncrasies and productions belong, in large measure, to the whole, which is made up of past as well as present, the latter pregnant with the future. Yet, though fed upon the elements (sometimes the refuse) of the past, each time seems to develop according to its own nature. Waywardly, foolishly, or with wholesome originality, it evolves a novel temperament and novel thoughts.

We shall treat the fifteenth and sixteenth centuries as a final and objective present; and all that went before will be regarded as a past which entered into them. It included pagan Antiquity, Judaism and the Gospel, the influence of the fecund East, the contribution of the Christian Fathers,—this whole store of knowledge and emotion, not merely as it came into being, but in its changing progress through the Middle Ages, until it entered the thought of our period and became the stimulus or suggestion of its feeling. Distinctive mediaeval creations likewise must be included, seeing that they also entered formatively into the constitutions of later men. The Middle Ages helped antiquity to shape the faculties and furnish the tastes of the sixteenth century. These faculties and tastes were then applied to what the past seemed also to offer as from a distinct and separate platform. Only by realizing the action of these formative and contributive agencies, shall we perceive this period's true relationships, and appreciate its caused and causal being, begotten of the past, yet vital (as each period is) with its own spirit, and big with a modernity which was not yet.

Two pasts may be distinguished, the one remote, the other proximate. The former may be taken as consisting of the antique world as it became its greater self, and then as it crumbled, while its thought and mood were assuming those forms in which they passed into the Middle Ages. The proximate or immediate past was the mediaeval time, itself progressing century after century under the influence of whatever had entered into it, chiefly through those last solvent and transition centuries in which the remote past ended.

The Middle Ages and the fifteenth or sixteenth century bore the same fundamental relationship to this remote past. Each succeeding mediaeval century, besides inheriting what had become known in the time directly preceding it, endeavored to reach back to the remote past for further treasure. Thus the twelfth century sought to reach behind the eleventh, in order to learn more of the greater past, and the thirteenth reached behind the twelfth. So Petrarch, in the fourteenth, would reach behind the vociferously damned thirteenth century to antiquity itself; and the fifteenth century humanists endeavored to do likewise. That century, like Petrarch's time, drew from its immediate mediaeval past as copiously as each mediaeval century drew from its predecessor, and *willy nilly* resembled the mediaeval centuries in striving to reach back of them for treasures previously undisclosed.

One thinks of the transmitted influence of the past, whether remote or proximate, as knowledge and suggestion, as intellectual or emotional or social material to be appropriated and made further use of. It is well to think of it also as flowing on in modes of expression, which constitute the finished form of the matter, whether the form lie in language or in the figures of plastic art. Thoughts and emotions cannot pass from one time to another save in modes of their expression. And the more finished and perfect, the more taking, the more beautiful, the form of expression, the more enduring will be its influence and effect. The seemingly formless material which is transmitted orally or in manuscripts or printed books from age to age, had necessarily reached some mode of expression, however vile. And although much wretched matter has come down through time, we may not ascribe its survival to the shortcomings of its form, but rather to the fact that somehow in its wretchedness and intellectual squalor it suited the squalid ignorance of men.

So it is fruitful to think, for instance, of each mediaeval century, as well as of the great sixteenth, as drawing the language of its thinking from the past, and then building up its own forms of thinking and expression. Each province of discipline furnishes concepts and a vocabulary. As each century appropriates them and makes them its own, they become its modes of thought, and the forms of its self-expression. Thus not only thought, but the language of expression, is handed on with enhancements from generation to generation. Each generation uses the thought, and expresses itself in the forms and concepts, which it has made its own—has made into its self-expression. Yet there is some change, some increase, some advance. To the transformation of inherited thought and phrase into modes of self-expression, each century or generation brings a tone and temper of its own, perhaps some change of attitude toward life, and at all events the increment and teaching of the experience which has come to it through living.

Difficulties of arrangement confront a work like the present. Shall it cleave to racehood and nationality or follow topics? Topics ignore racial lines and geographical boundaries.

The plan must bend to the demands on it. Sometimes racial traits dominate an individual, and the conditions of his life and land shape his career, even a great career like Luther's. A national situation may point the substance of an issue, as, in England, in Wyclif's controversy with the papacy. For quite another illustration, one may observe how a diversity of interest and taste between Italians and Frenchmen impressed a different purpose and manner upon classical studies in Italy and France.

On the other hand such a story as that of the advance of the physical sciences in the fifteenth and sixteenth centuries has little to do with land or race; the votaries belong to every people, and pursue their investigations indifferently in their own countries or where foreign localities offer greater advantages. So a general survey should follow the course of the most dominant and vital elements.

A kindred question goes to the roots of the truth of phenomena: should one adhere to a temporal arrangement, century by century, or follow sequences of influence and effect across the imaginary boundaries of these arbitrary time divisions? While it is convenient to speak of "centuries," one is always pursuing the vital continuity of effect. The virtue of fruitful effort passes into future achievement. One seeks to follow facts in their progeny. Yet this is difficult, since the genealogical tree is infinitely ramified, and every event, every achievement, has as many forbears as a human being! The truthfulness of events lies in the process of *becoming*, rather than in the concrete phenomenon which catches our attention. It would be as foolish to end the consideration of Petrarch with his death as it would be to treat him as if he and his work and influence really began the day when he was born, or first read Cicero. Nothing begins or ends. We may even think of all that is, or ever was or will be, as one mighty self-evolving present, which holds the effective being, the becoming, of the past, and contains the future, of which this present is in turn the becoming.

HENRY OSBORN TAYLOR

New York, May, 1920.

Erasmus and Luther

Chapter 1

Scholarship in Germany and the Netherlands

WHETHER IN HER TIMES of mental squalor or her times of brilliancy, Italy was reminiscent of her past and sensitive to its influence. Classic literature and art were for her an expression of a greater pagan manhood, once hers and still having silent part in whatever her people might achieve. It was natural that a renewed and broader reading of the Classics and a more facile imitation of the ancient buildings and the ancient sculptures should be the chief element in her intellectual and catholic progress in the fourteenth and following centuries.

But the Roman past was not the source of all intellectual elements in the North. The northern peoples had their own potent antecedents. They were not the direct descendants of the Romans, but, at most, spiritual collaterals with other strains of blood. Their past had been monastic and feudal, rather than secular and urban. Monasticism had scant sympathy for the classics, and feudalism had developed a taste for turbulent epics and adventurous romance. The North had looked on the classics as a store of knowledge; and northern intellectual energies, focussing at last in the University of Paris, devoted themselves to a most unhumanistic exploitation of ancient philosophy in scholasticism and mediaeval science, false or true. Christianity itself as understood and developed or corrupted in the North had but loose kinship with the Latin paganism which underlay the religiousness of Italy. The northern religion held Celtic and Teutonic heathen elements, unhumanistic and unmalleable. It proved more unyielding to the influence of pagan humanism than the Christianity of Italy.

Nevertheless, the Latin language and the great works composed in it had been the vehicle of educational discipline in France and Germany and England. And in those countries as well as in Italy, the classics offered human wisdom and a broad consideration of life to whoever might read and partially understand them.

Accordingly when, under suggestions from the passionate classical revival in Italy, the peoples of the north turned to the classics with a renewed and deeper zeal, their purpose was not confined to improvement in education and Latinity. The intentions and desires of the northern humanists were as broad as their own natures, and their natures were developing with the study of this humanizing literature. Their pursuits were an expression of their wish for a more humane, a more rational and reasonable, treatment of life. Clearly the growing interest in the classics and the broadening of the purpose of their study was part of the general intellectual and social development, and a moving factor in the same.

The whole matter is illustrated by the career and function and effect of the northern apostle of humanism and reasonableness, Desiderius Erasmus. Since all classes in the north were keenly interested in their religion, the labors of Erasmus were naturally directed to the scholarly study of the New Testament and the Church Fathers as well as to a better understanding of the pagan classics. What is true of the great Erasmus is true of northern scholars before him as well as those who felt his influence. And with them, as with their leader, classical studies were part of a more instructed appreciation of what was rational, and of what was irrational, absurd or intolerable, not merely in social life but in religious doctrine and practice. Humanism became an early factor in the coming religious revolution, from which it was destined later to part company in Germany and France and England.

In the Low Countries, where Erasmus was a native, as well as in the Germany educationally affiliated with them, there had been educational and intellectual progress in the fourteenth century. Stimulus usually would come, or seem to come, from some person gifted with energy, vision, or initiative, above his fellows. Toward the close of the century an influence making for the diffusion of a better education sprang from Gerard Groot, founder of the *Brothers of the Common Life* at his home city of Deventer, in the northeastern part of what now is Holland. He had been a vigorous preacher against the lusts of the clergy; and it was a simple teaching and preaching fraternity that he founded, composed of men who inclined toward evangelical piety, yet were obedient to the Church, and had no revolutionary aims. They were not bound by monastic vows; they taught the poor *gratis,* and preached in the vernacular, urging those who could not read Latin to read the Bible in their own tongue. On the other hand, they advocated frequent reference to the original texts in order to correct errors in the Vulgate. They spoke little of dogmas in their sermons.

One senses a certain freedom of the spirit among these Brethren, with a perception of the religious and educational elements which soon were to be recognized as cardinal. One also sees in them a tendency toward a purer Gospel faith, and an effort to better the lives of clergy and laity. Groot died in 1384, still in the prime of life. Able coadjutors remained; and Deventer became the home of pious and sensible education. The Brethren extended their labors, and opened schools at many places in the Low Countries, the influence of which reached the neighboring parts of Germany. These schools attracted capable teachers and pupils, and seemed to develop the talents both of those who taught and those who studied in them. The numbers were great, and the list of names is impressive. Thomas à Kempis, born near Cologne, was one of the

Brethren; and Nicholas of Cusa, whose intellectual power was unequalled in his time, studied at Deventer.

Rudolf Agricola touched this circle, and Hegius was very part of it. The former, a Frisian, born in 1442, studied at Deventer and Louvain, and then spent several years in Italy completing his classical equipment. Returning to Germany, he devoted himself to translating the old German chronicles and diffusing a knowledge of the classics. He did not fail in Christian piety, and held to the idea that all learning should serve the Faith. He died in 1485.

Of about the same age as Agricola was the Westphalian Hegius, who chose to call himself his pupil and became Deventer's greatest schoolmaster. He had been a pupil with the Brethren, and in middle life fixed himself at Deventer, where he taught from 1475 until his death in 1498. A man of unquestioned piety, he was also a scholar and knew Greek. He improved the methods of teaching, replaced the old text books by better ones, and made a study of the classics the centre of his curriculum. Pupils came to him from near and far, till his school numbered above two thousand. His crown of praise lay in the names of those who called him master. Erasmus was among them.

We turn from the Brethren and their pupils to a famous German educator who in no way belonged to them, the Alsatian Wimpheling. Born in 1450, he first studied at Freiburg, where the old *Doctrinale* was his grammar. Next at Erfurt, where he touched the new humanism, but only to be drawn back to Heidelberg, whose university was still threshing the old scholastic straw and little else. Disgusted with the Canon Law, to which he had been destined, he felt various currents drawing him to *belles lettres* and verse-making, to public questions, and to religion, for he too was looking for salvation. He became a bachelor of Theology in 1483; but instead of following that vocation, turned to teaching the sadly needed humanities at Heidelberg. The futility of the dispute as to universals became with him a favorite topic of discourse. Later in life, he went to Strassburg, and there rather vainly undertook to establish better schools. He did not die till 1528. His life and somewhat confused labors at least evince serious endeavors for a better scheme of education, for the diffusion of liberal knowledge, and a reform of the morals of the clergy. The writings of this occasionally bitter disputant were effective and popular. They laid bare the absurdities of current ways of education, and presented rational methods of teaching the ancient languages, and training the intelligence and character of pupils.

The lives of these men covered the period of the invention of printing, or more specifically speaking, of the art of casting metal type. Wimpheling said truthfully that the Germans could so justly pride themselves over no other invention of the mind. From the year 1462, when the secret process was divulged at Maintz, presses were established rapidly through Germany, and in Italy and France. Printing was hailed as a portentous event, for good or evil. It was indeed the main title of the Germans to intellectual fame. They might respect themselves for the improvement of their education and their progress in classical studies; yet so far there was small matter in one or the other to attract the praise or attention of other peoples, Italians, French, English or Lowlanders. The historian who is not a German will trace without enthusiasm the advent and progress of the new waves of humanism. "Educators of Germany," arose, a title given to Rabanus Maurus in the ninth century, and now to be shared by Wimpheling with the younger man, Melanchthon, and perhaps others. But these educators of Germany were not like the Italian humanists, educators of the world. The one man who rightly won a towering fame was not a German, but Erasmus of Rotterdam.

The classics had not been left unread in mediaeval Germany, but the taste of the thirteenth and fourteenth centuries turned to a scholastic exploitation of Aristotelian logic and metaphysics, with some incursions into the antique field of physical science. The renewed interest in the classics, appearing here and there in the fifteenth century,

usually carried a lively detestation of the methods and topics of scholasticism, which still occupied the universities.
But this reaction did not spring from any such natural disposition toward antique humanism as marked the Italian
mind. There had been no substratum of antique civilization
in Germany, a land never subjected to the transforming discipline of the imperial Roman order. The German past had
been that of Teutonic barbarism, with its hard heathen
religion. Next, Germany became feudal and monastic,
still unsuited to the urban antique humanism. What city
life there was remained dull and uninstructed far into the
fifteenth century. Moreover, although the Germans showed
few signs of becoming a nation, they had attained a stub-
born racial character, which would hardly yield itself to
alien moulds. They had, to be sure, been ready to accept
literary and social fashions, for example from the French
side of the Rhine; but they had sturdily remained Germans; and now were to prove again in the fifteenth and
sixteenth centuries that they could take up the study of
Latin and Greek literature, and interest themselves in
the Italian humanism, without imperilling their German
natures. It held true as a corollary that they would use
the new knowledge according to their own convictions and
abiding interests. German scholars did not become humanists after the Italian fashion, bent solely upon absorbing the
classics; but rather they sought to apply the new knowledge to the conditions of life in Germany and the problems
of the approaching religious unheaval. Least of all, did
German scholarship attempt an artistic or creative imitation of the classics, as the Italians did; but earnestly
studied the Greek and Latin languages and endeavored
to obtain a solid understanding of their literatures.

Stimulus and suggestion came from Italy. For example,
the chancellor of the Emperor Karl IV, Johann von Neu-
markt, who flourished between 1350 and 1375, drew an
inflated inspiration from Petrarch. In the next generation,
another German thinks Salutato the wonder of scholars,
and seeks his acquaintance in Florence. Soon the Emperor

Sigismund was to feel a lively interest in the literature, the history, the ruins of antiquity, and become a patron of Italian humanists. Then incitement to antique studies came from Italy in the person of Aeneas Silvius, ardent humanist, clever diplomat, future cardinal, and at last Pope.[1] He did his best to infuse a love of letters into these northern swine, as he deemed them; but the result fell short of his wishes. His race and personality roused distrust in the German bosom. We see the antipathy toward him concentrate in Gregor Heimburg, jurist and statesman, and most emphatic German, whom Aeneas by no blandishment could win either to his policy or his friendship. This able speaker professed to despise the artifices of rhetoric and all Italianate imitation of the ancients.

Study of the classics did not shake the piety of German students in the fifteenth century, whose names and particular accomplishments need not be catalogued. An earlier generation was succeeded by those born in decades when the German people were entering a period of religious and political conflict. These younger men were affected by the controversies of the time, and some of them caught by its whirlwinds. Naturally they used their faculties and inclined the fruit of their studies to timely ends.

One may make one's approach to the years of larger conflict through the achievements and troubles of the most distinguished German scholar of his time, Johann Reuchlin.[2] Born in Pforzheim, the gate of the Black Forest, in 1455, he studied for a while at Freiburg, and then made his way to Paris, where he learned some Greek. He went next to Basel and then to Paris again, to learn more Greek. But having chosen jurisprudence as his profession, he turned his steps to Orleans. He had become a teacher now, of Latin and Greek, and as such went to Tübingen at the close of the year 1481. There the patronage of the

---

1 Aeneas Silvius Piccolomini was born near Sienna in 1405. He went to the Council of Basel in 1432; and afterwards was much at Vienna and elsewhere in Germany. He became Pope Pius II in 1458, and died in 1464.

2 See L. Geiger, *Johann Reuchlin*, (Leipsic 1871).

great came upon him, and within a few months he was taken to Italy by the Count of Würtemberg. So he made the acquaintance of Italian humanists, and impressed them with his Greek. It was, however, on a later Italian journey that he met Pico della Mirandola. This may have inspired him to take up the study of Hebrew and the Cabbala, as he did under the guidance of learned Jews. Reuchlin moved with people of station: as a man, as a publicist, as a scholar, he was honored by all. The list of his writings opens with a brief Latin Dictionary, produced at the age of twenty. In course of time, he wrote Latin verses and comedies, some of the last apparently in imitation of a French model. He made Latin translations from the Greek; Homer's *Battle of the Frogs and Mice* and some treatises of Athanasius were among them, and denote his range.

All this was respectable. But Reuchlin's service to scholarship was his work in Hebrew. His *Rudamenta hebraica* laid the foundations of its study among the Germans. He did not stop, however, with scholarly and unquestionably meritorious work upon the languages; but chose to follow the venturesome Pico into the caves of the Cabbala, which held nostrums of blessedness not found so clearly in the Old Testament. Like Pico he took from it according to his taste. Rejecting its sorcery and astrology, he made his own its equally wonderful wisdom, which linked man with his beatitude. The "wonder working word" he made the title of his book, *De Verbo mirifico*. This was followed by further seductive exposition in his *De Arte Cabalistica;* which appeared in 1517, when Luther was already holding forth other matters!

Troubles fell on Reuchlin. The Vulgate was the authoritative sacred vehicle of truth; and to many churchmen Hebrew and Greek scholarship, with its appeal to the original texts, was irritating and disturbing. So Erasmus learned when he had edited the Greek New Testament, and so Reuchlin might learn from the fortunes of his Hebrew grammar. Some people likewise looked askance on his ponderous flirtation with the Cabbala. Such were the suspect fringes of his great repute, when partly through the force of circumstances, and partly through his self-respect, he became the centre of a struggle for the freedom of scholarship. A preposterous converted Jew named Pfeffercorn, with malignant eagerness to convert his stiff-necked people, obtained a decree from the Emperor Maximilian authorizing him to find and destroy those Jewish books which were hostile to the Christian faith. He was supported by the Dominicans of the Cologne university. A bitter and most elaborate and complicated controversy followed. The universities gave their opinions. Reuchlin was drawn in, and showed himself the champion of the Jewish books; for he held the cause of scholarship, as well as true religion, to be involved. The Dominicans brought charges of heresy against him and his writings. The cause, tried once and again in Germany, was decided there in Reuchlin's favor; and the Dominicans appealed to Rome, where, after years, a halting decision was rendered. That did not end it. The matter was still fought out in Germany, and even in other lands. The scholar humanists were Reuchlin's partisans, with many a good reactionary on the other side. A few years before Reuchlin's death, his grand-nephew Philip Melanchthon, a prodigy of precocious scholarship, was called to Wittenberg, and the great uncle sent him with his blessing. The Lutheran revolt was already moving briskly with great noise. The venerable Reuchlin, like many another humanist of his generation, drew back from it and died within the bosom of the church.

If Reuchlin's cause was won, it was won by wit and laughter, quite as much as by more solemn means. Wit's best contribution to the fray was from the humanists of Erfurt, aided by the redoubtable Ulrich von Hutten. It was a vicious kind of confetti, these *Epistolae Obscurorum Virorum*, written in the funniest hog-Latin. The fun carries sheer across the centuries, and stirs to laughter yet. The Cologne Dominicans could never pick these burrs out of their hides.[3]

3 There is an admirable edition of the *Epistolae Obscurorum Virorum*, with introduction and English translation by F. G. Stokes (London 1909).

A leader of the Erfurt humanists was one Konrad Mut, called Mutianus Rufus, or, less euphoniously, the red-haired. Though not shown to have contributed to the *Letters of the Obscure,* he wrote many of his own, through which he remains noticeable, if not notable. He will answer for a closing example of the German humanist of Erasmus's generation.

Born at Homberg in 1471, he too studied under Hegius at Deventer. He came to Erfurt in 1486 and is found teaching there in 1492. Three years later he set out for Italy, travelled through its cities and listened to the humanists, Pico and Ficino among others. He did not return to Germany till 1502. He tried official life, abandoned it, and built himself a little house in Gotha, near the Cathedral. Inscribing *Beata Tranquillitas* upon the door in golden letters, he settled himself within, and lived there till his death in 1526.

Mutianus was a cultivated man, devoted to carrying out his tastes. The classics were his chief love, as scholasticism, according to the humanistic convention, was his abomination. He had a good knowledge of the Civil Law, and held, with the new school of jurists, that one should study the *Corpus Juris* itself, and not the commentators. He was not unread in medicine and Pliny; had a mild belief in astrology, but rejected magic.

Naturally he was a partisan of Reuchlin. But Erasmus was his idol, in scholarship and in attitude toward life. He saw in him the restorer of theology and the font from which Œcolampadius, Luther, and Melanchthon drew.[4] This was the view of many. As a follower of Erasmus, Mutianus took a rational or rationalistic view of religion, going a little further than his model, or at all events expressing thoughts which Erasmus would have disavowed. Indeed he strikes us as one of those paganizers whom Erasmus disapproved in his *Ciceronianus.*[5] One God or

[4] As in Epistle to Lang, (1520) printed p. 641 of C. Krause, *Briefwechsel des Mutianus Rufus* (Kassel, 1885): with a full introduction.
[5] See Chap. 2.

Goddess, *Natura,* he would adore under many names or manifestations—*nomina* or *numina.* They included the old Pantheon, to which Moses and Christ should be added. "When I say Jupiter, I mean Christ and the true God." Of course, Mutianus finds a Christianity before Christ, whose humanity he regarded merely as a semblance. "The true Christ is soul and spirit, not to be handled with the hands." So he interpreted Christianity loosely and easily, discarding, for example, the resurrection of the body. His wit hovered on the edge of irreverence.

This man of scholarly habit, who disliked tumult as much as Erasmus did, drew back from Luther, of whom at first he approved. He preferred books and a rational life; and like Erasmus, he found himself rather solitary in his closing years, having declined the conflict in which his countrymen were engaged. Yet he held himself a good German, read books in his native tongue and professed a high regard for at least the possibilities of German culture.

So we are brought back to the fact that the German humanists were emphatically Germans; they held themselves as German patriots, and evinced not infrequently an active interest in the history and literature of Germany. Kaiser Max set the fashion, and German princes imitated his patronage of studies, which threw light on the German past and enhanced the Fatherland's repute. Here humanist patricians, leaders in their cities, like Wilibald Pirckheimer of Nuremberg or Conrad Peutinger of Augsburg, vied with scholars of private station, like Celtis or Beatus Rhenanus. Or one may name Trithemius, abbot of Sponheim near Kreuznach, reformer of his Order, and founder of something like a learned Academy. He was perhaps the first to outline a history of German literature. A different and more tempestuous German patriot will be found in Ulrich von Hutten, who will cry aloud for mention when we come to speak of the German hatred of the Italian papacy.

Before leaving Germany proper, one notes the hostility of Cologne and other universities to the newer better learning. This fact was by no means peculiar to Germany.

The hostility of the established faculties at Louvain will drive Erasmus to abandon his attempt to establish there a college for the study of Greek, Hebrew and Latin. In France, the attitude of the Sorbonne, that is, the theological faculty of the University of Paris, was even more malignantly reactionary. As the fifteenth century passes into the sixteenth, the Sorbonne became suspicious of the slightest change in institution or opinion, and was quick to crush any attempt for the reform of education or the advancement of learning. Rightly they felt that light from any side might imperil their position. Many a French scholar sought a freer air in the large provincial cities like Lyons, or found it at the court of Margaret of Navarre.[6] Likewise in Germany learning was cultivated by individual scholars apart from universities, or in liberal minded circles in the great commercial cities of Strassburg, Augsburg or Nuremberg. The routes of commerce brought the good things of the spirit too, and the wealth of the leading burghers was turned to the patronage of art and letters.

Looking now more particularly to the Netherlands, one notes the general establishment of printing presses between the years 1473 and 1491. As in Germany so in the Netherlands, the diffusion of knowledge, and especially of the new humanism, was facilitated and encouraged through the new art of printing. Deventer was among the first to have its press (1476). And with Deventer and the Brethren of the Common Life one recalls that the currents of school education overran political boundaries.

Yet there was a difference between German and Netherland scholars, and between the purposes to which they applied their culture. The Germans, as remarked, were enthusiastic, sometimes rampant, Germans; the scholars of the Low Countries had no corresponding passion. Theirs was not a great self-conscious country, feeling its racehood perhaps the more acutely through despair of political union. The Netherlands had no such hope. This little country had been a battle ground for rival potentates

[6] See Chaps. 3 and 7.

whose homes were elsewhere; politically it seemed doomed to be an appanage of Burgundy, of Austria, of Spain. It had no national tongue; but hung divided between Dutch, Flemish and French. Territorial pride and intellectual energy did not unite in the creation of a national literature. The country was too small; its people too few. It was a highway of commerce and ideas; the people had industrial and commercial aptitude; their cities were as factories and marts, open to the traffic of the world. Thought and scholarship were not impressed with local aims or national ambitions, nor provincialized through patriotism. Till persecution came, there was nothing to prevent acceptance of whatever might present universal human interest and validity.[7]

It may be remarked that an advance in sacred studies usually accompanied the progress of classical scholarship. There were efforts in the Middle Ages to reach a closer understanding of the Scriptures than could be had from the Vulgate, which a few scholars dared to say was sometimes faulty in its renderings. To this end at Cambridge in the thirteenth century, Robert Grosseteste and Roger Bacon planned and labored to revive a knowledge of Hebrew and of Greek.[8] The result of their labors did not perish, but continued, trickling in hidden currents, which now and then rose to the surface in the work of some man we know. Such a one was Nicholas of Lyra in the diocese of Evreux, where he was born toward the close of the thirteenth century. He became a Franciscan monk, and died about the middle of the next century. He acquired a considerable knowledge of both Greek and Hebrew and was a good Biblical scholar, writing brief commentaries upon the Scriptures, and a much needed work distinguishing the canonical from the Apocryphal books. As a commentator his chief and rather individual merit was that he tried to ascertain the actual meaning of the text, and did

7 Cf. H. Pirenne, *Histoire de Belgique*, t. III. pp. 285 sqq. (1907).

8 See *The Mediaeval Mind*, chap. XXXI.

not abandon himself to the conventional allegorical interpretations.[9]

In Italy the fifteenth century brought a reviving interest in Christian letters, especially in the works of the great fourth and fifth century doctors. Even earlier Christian writings occasionally appear in the large libraries, as that of Pope Nicholas V (1447-55) and that of Niccolo Niccoli, the Florentine, who died in 1437. Christian letters owed much to the labors of Niccolo's friend, Ambrogio Traversari, both as a collector of manuscripts, and as a painful translator from the Greek.[10] Lorenzo Valla, most critical of Italian scholars, exposer of the forgery of the "Donation of Constantine," was a younger contemporary of these men. In the next generation comes the Florentine, Ficino, who lectured upon Paul as well as Plato, and whose influence may have suggested the famous lectures which were given at Oxford about the year 1500 by Colet, Dean of St. Paul's, a liberal and intelligent Christian scholar, a friend of Thomas More and Erasmus. All three were bent upon applying the resources of the new scholarship to the interpretation of Christian documents, and their best intelligence to an understanding of the faith. Their friends and admirers, especially those of Erasmus, were so great in number and so conspicuous in attainments and influence, as to constitute a party in favor of a rational and considerably reformed Catholic religion. Colet and More will come before us hereafter. We turn now to Erasmus who presents the culmination of this revival of Christian scholarship in the North, and a good deal besides.

[9] See Altmeyer, *Les Précurseurs de la Réforme aux Pays-Bas,* vol. I. pp. 99-101 (The Hague, 1886). I wish to express my indebtedness to the admirable chapter entitled "The Christian Renaissance" by M. R. James, in vol. I. of *The Cambridge Modern History.* Cf. also P. Wernle, *Die Renaissance des Christentums im 16. Jahrhundert* (1904).

[10] Cf. Vol. I, Chap. 2.

Chapter 2

Desiderius Erasmus, the Northern
Apostle of Letters and Reasonableness

ERASMUS WAS THE MOST influential man of letters of his
time and the most catholic in the scope of his pursuits. He
was the universal humanist, not merely following the profession of humane letters but inculcating their lessons of
reasonableness in his writings and his life. And as he ex-
emplified the northern tendency toward erudition and at
the same time cultivated the elegances of composition as
aptly as any Italian, he combined the intellectual charac-
teristics noticeable on opposite sides of the Alps.

He happened to be born in Holland,[1] which was one
reason why he was an unattached citizen of the world—
the world of letters. Many of his later years were passed at
Basel, where he died in 1536. Basel was a chief city in a
small country divided in race and language, religion and
politics. Erasmus was attracted by the absence of national
obsessions, as well as by the facilities afforded there for
the printing of his books. But he felt at home wherever he
was comfortable, had the food and wine which suited him,
found congenial friends, was let alone to work, and left

[1] The year was 1466. The facts of Erasmus's life as far as
known, and a little further, may be left to the numerous biogra-
phies, and introductions to his various works. P. S. Allen's *Age of
Erasmus* is a summary by one whose knowledge of Erasmus's life
and letters is unequalled. Several volumes of Allen's edition of the
letters have appeared. I should also refer to F. M. Nichol's *Epistles
of Erasmus,* 2 vols. in translations (Longmans 1901) and E.
Emerton's *Life of Erasmus,* (New York, Putnams, 1899).

33

unmolested by religious strife. Of uncertain health and delicate physique, he required a considerable income for his comfort; and was importunate and industrious in obtaining it. He insisted upon freedom of movement and occupation; ties and obligations, such as regular teaching at a university, were intolerable to him. He belonged to no country, was untouched by national prejudices, hates, or aspirations, social, political, or religious. Void of racial sympathy and antipathy, detesting partisanship, except that making for intellectual enlightenment, he would link himself to no revolutionary movement nor to the reactionary powers seeking to suppress it. The one or the other might imperil the advance of letters and true piety. Reckoning wrongly with the power, even the power of advance, which lies in passionate rejection, he held to the futile hope of purifying and rationalizing Catholicism, without breaking its unity. Yet his efforts to incorporate in religion the spirit and certified results of the best scholarship, bore fruit. Of course he did not realize that the will to remake the Church represented the most intense phase of the northern desire for truth, a desire heated by antagonism to Rome and empassioned with yearning for unmediated union with the saving grace of God.

The moving sincerities of Erasmus, and the motives of his conduct, appear in the very things in which he was thought a dissembler. His was a rational and penetrating intelligence; a strong and educated common sense. He had the gift of seeing the point, the veritable principle: for example, that virtue lies in good intent and corresponding conduct, and not in the letter of the indifferent and superstitious observance. He saw the lack of essential connection between such observance and spiritual betterment. If this had been perceived by men before him, from the time when Isaiah reported that Jehovah would have righteousness and not sacrifice, nevertheless Erasmus saw for himself, with a renewed and timely insight, the silliness and brutishness of the current religious and social life. He would apply an informed intelligence to the improvement of education, the betterment of society, the purification of religion. As the fanatic impulse was not his, he had no wish to destroy whatever might be harmlessly retained in the established order of religion, government, or daily living. Enlightenment based on scholarship was his aim for himself and for society. In religion, as in secular culture, this pious, but not extravagantly religious, man loved the truth that was definite and tangible, and had no taste for the mystic or metaphysical. The ethical element appealed to him more than the theological. He wished to establish and publish the most authentic Christian record, which for him set forth the surest religious truth. Hence he spent a good part of his life and strength in editing the texts of Holy Scripture and the accredited Fathers of the Church.

At the same time Erasmus was always a wit, a litterateur, a professional author of prodigious facility and artistic temperament. He was drawn to the artistically admirable in life as well as literature. He could not complacently endure physical discomforts, or the incongruous or disagreeable in his relations with other men. With him the pressing trouble was apt to give shape and color to a situation, which he might then set forth plausibly and even self-deceptively, so as to accredit himself, dispel his annoyance, or present a means of escape. Not infrequently he sees his relations to other men as he would have them, and as he thought they should be. His supple epistolary faculty lent itself to the subconscious, or sometimes conscious, manipulation of fact. Just as in his youth he had been addicted to the over-expression of friendship; which is one way of idealizing actual relationships and apprehending them as they should preciously be, but not quite as they are, and certainly not as they endure.

This scholar-artist passed three years in Italy when Leonardo, Michelangelo, and Raphael were at their zenith; his own portrait was painted many times by the greatest of German painters. He was himself an observer of *moeurs*. Yet as with many supremely bookish people, his writings show small interest in art outside of literature. Even in literature, he had little taste for poetry. He was not gifted with the emotionally impelled imagination of the poetic faculty. His imagination was entirely rational. Even in religion he apprehended rationally, not with quick intuitions; and entertained no feelings, experiences, convictions, which he could not rationally explain and justify.

There is no need to worry because the letters of Erasmus show flaws of character, shared with many other humanists: readiness to flatter for money, querulous fault-finding, a tendency to abuse those whom he had unsuccessfully adulated. Why insist upon staunchness of character in a man of letters, who is a lover of learning and rational enlightenment, and a sincere commender of sensible and pious conduct? Erasmus's strength lay in the genius which responded to these desires, and boldly enough displayed itself in the witty and purposeful presentation of the ridiculous and the rational, the degraded and the intelligent, and from a like point of view, the evil and the good. There was enough strength of character in his will, which kept him free to pursue his scholar-quest of knowledge, even truth, and through a long life, set it forth in books.

One may say that the central purpose of the life and labors of Erasmus was to get an education, and enable others to obtain one. To this end, the first step, taken or forced upon him in his youth, was an acquaintance with the current methods and knowledge included in the curriculum of elementary and university teaching. He absorbed this discipline with a conscious acceptance of some of its principles, and an irritated rejection of others. Those processes of acceptance and rejection included religious as well as secular education. They extended through Erasmus's long apprentice years, and, in the nature of things, never were concluded. On such foundations he built the higher stages of his education, which led on through improving the educational apparatus of his early years, through acquiring further knowledge, and through presenting with novel insight whatever he had learned.

Judged by Erasmus's standards, the schools of the closing fifteenth century were backward in methods and textbooks. The barbarous *Graecismus* of the twelfth century was dictated to Erasmus at Deventer. A rather better grammar, likewise metrical, the *Doctrinale* of Alexander de Ville-Dieu, was still in universal use. The scholarly bent of the masters of Deventer seems not to have affected the routine of the school. Erasmus studied under them from his eleventh to his eighteenth year. He next spent two years at the school of the Brethren of the Common Life at Bois-le-Duc; and then, impelled by circumstances, he entered as a novice the house of the Augustinian canons at Stein, near Gouda, where he remained for seven or eight years, and took the vows. Later, he inveighed against the barbarous and monkish education of this period of his life. Yet at Stein he studied the Latin classics and occupied himself fruitfully with the *Elegantiae* of Valla, making an epitome of it. He could have found no better compend of the newer classical scholarship.

Erasmus had progressed notably in learning by the year 1493, when at the age of twenty-seven he was taken from Stein by the Bishop of Cambrai, and two years afterwards sent to study theology at Paris, where he was entered in the malodorous College of Montaigu. His contempt deepened for the "Scotists," and for scholastic philosophy which they seemed to symbolize. So he cultivated the classics as best he might, and also taught. He thus fell in with a number of Englishmen, among them his pupil-patron, Lord Mountjoy, whom he accompanied to England in 1499, where he became the friend of Thomas More and John Colet, to the lasting pleasure and advantage of the three. At Oxford, Colet suggested lectures on the Old Testament, to supplement those novel discourses on the Epistles of Paul with which he was then stirring the University.[2] Erasmus's antipathy to current scholastic ways of treating Scripture needed no goad. But he became

2 See Vol. IV, Chap. 1.

acutely conscious of the need of Greek for one who would be a New Testament scholar. As Oxford possessed little Greek, he returned to Paris to resume its study.

Greek concluded the predominantly acquisitive stage of Erasmus's education. He studied it without instructors or the modern apparatus of dictionary and grammar. By the year 1506, when he was no longer young, he had made such progress as to embolden him afterwards to assert that he learned nothing from his sojourn in Italy, which extended from that year to 1509. There was a Frenchman, named Budé, who could still have taught him, and doubtless did, since the two became frequent correspondents, if not friends. As the years increased Erasmus's fame, he did not evince a genial spirit towards his great rival for the primacy of European scholarship.

The education of Erasmus, as with all intelligent people, continued through his life. The acquisitive phases were always interwoven with his critical development and conscious rejection of much that he had previously been taught. To these educational processes of learning, criticism and rejection, were joined his more productive activities, which also were to be educational for himself as for the student world. These extended back into his acquisitive period, and on through his entire life.

This most effective educator of northern Europe spent little time teaching in universities. In consequence his influence, his effect, was tenfold greater. Unhampered and undulled, he gave his entire strength to scholarship and the making of books which were of enormous educational effect. In them one can follow—if one has sufficient leisure! —the cumulative self-expression of the author. They are of endless bulk, ten large folios in the Leyden edition. Had Erasmus written less, he might be more read today. But that would signify little. His writings are not needed now; they tell us mostly things we either know or have forgotten to our advantage. But they were needed in their time, and were found neither too many nor too long. They were serviceable to the people of Germany and France and

England in the sixteenth century, and contained much matter which it was well at that time to bring to men's attention.

Among the formal educational treatises of Erasmus, the *De Ratione Studii*,[3] written in 1511 at Colet's request, presents a plan for imparting to the pupil something of the wisdom of the Ancients, which embraced all knowledge: "omnis fere rerum scientia a Graecis auctoribus petenda est";—one need not be suprised at mediaeval echoes in Erasmus's writings.[4] The teacher, says he, should learn the contents of the classics and arrange their matter in his note books, that he may impart it methodically. If he lacks a full library, he will find Pliny most rich in information, and next to him Macrobius, Aulus Gellius and Athenaeus. But he must "seek the *fontes ipsos,* to wit, the old Greeks. Plato best teaches philosophy, and Aristotle, and his disciple Theophrastus, and Plotinus, made up of them both. In Christian theology none is better than Origen, none more subtil than Chrysostom, none holier than Basil." The Latin Fathers Ambrose and Jerome are recommended, and other authors for various reasons.

Erasmus was well on in his sixties when he wrote an educational tract which laid intelligent stress on the need of beginning the boy's education very early, and under the most competent masters, who should employ methods

[3] Leyden edition of Erasmus's *Opera,* Tome I, fo. 521-530. I have used to advantage W. H. Woodward's *Desiderius Erasmus concerning the aim and method of Education* (Cambridge 1904), which also gives a translation of this treatise and the *De Pueris Instituendis*. I cannot but think that Prof. Woodward might have made his translations somewhat closer to Erasmus's language, and have been less free in the use of modern educational phrases, which represent concepts not current in the sixteenth century.

[4] Sometimes he uses exactly the mediaeval phrase, as in his letter dedicating the first edition of the *Adagia* to Lord Mountjoy: "Accordingly, laying aside all serious labors, and indulging in a more dainty kind of study, I strolled through the gardens provided by various authors, culling as I went the adages most remarkable for their antiquity and excellence, like so many flowers of various sorts, of which I have made a nosegay." F. M. Nichol's translation.

of gentleness and understanding, rather than those of violence and fear. This was the *De pueris ad virtutem ac literas liberaliter instituendis idque protinus a nativitate*.[5] One notes the last words of the title—"from their very birth." An uneducated man is not a *man; institutio* or training is more important than *natura*. Here man differs from the dumb animals.

> "whose protection nature has set in their inborn faculties; but since divine providence has bestowed the power of reason on man alone, it has left the chief share to training (Efficax res est natura, sed hanc vincit efficacior institutio). When nature gave thee a son, she delivered nothing but a *rudem massam*. It is for thee to impress the best character upon this submissive plastic material. If thou art remiss, thou wilt have a wild beast, but if vigilant, a divinity."

This treatise is not all wisdom. Erasmus gives, apparently from his favorite Pliny, plenty of absurd examples of what man may learn from brutes. And he says that boyhood's proneness to depravity, which so puzzled the ancients, is due to Adam's sin. But one will not ignore the fault of bad early training, he adds, perhaps with a submerged smile. He is clear as to the abomination of spoiling a child by indulgence and bad example; and shows how foolish it is to leave youth to acquire by experience such practical knowledge as might properly be taught.

For the rest, the treatise intelligently anticipates many of the demands of modern enlightenment touching juvenile education; for example the need to consider the disposition and faculties of each child. As a parent should instil in his child reverence and love, rather than fear, so in the boy's education, intelligent kindness and encouragement, not flogging, are the means to be employed. The very best and most scholarly men should be selected for

5 Published in 1529,—Leyden Ed. I, fo. 489-516. Translated by Woodward.

schoolmasters. There is no more important function. A teacher should not be too old; indeed he should become a boy again, that he may be loved by the boy. If he understands boy nature he will not treat his pupil like an uneducated little old man.

Erasmus speaks of suitable primary studies. Among them is language, which may be taught through pleasant fables, and by bringing the boy up among good talkers. There are hints for modern kindergartens, summed up in the recognition of the need to adapt the teaching to the child's nature. The closing paragraphs criticise the methods then pursued, and deride the still more wretched instruction of Erasmus's boyhood, when he learned Latin grammar through the repetition of absurd distiches, and wasted precious time in the labyrinth of dialectic. So, through ignorant teachers, the critical years of life are thrown away! His words echo the endless wail over the teaching of children;—teaching by rote, learning by rote; not easy to avoid even by enlightened modernity, and perhaps having some disciplinary value.

Erasmus descended more nearly to the needs of pupils in his *De Copia*,[6] a book to assist young people to acquire a Latin style. Admirable are its generalities: when and how to enrich, or condense, the expression of one's thoughts, while avoiding repetition in the one case, or an inept bareness in the other. The need of something to say is pointed out, as well as the need of a scholarly command of Latin to clothe one's thought. Erasmus proceeds, usefully and drearily, to a mass of detail and example which make the work a store of varied classical phrase and circumlocution. At Colet's solicitation weighted with coin, Erasmus dedicated it to the use of his friend's foundation, St. Paul's school. It proved a wonderful schoolbook and was republished sixty times in Erasmus's lifetime, and afterwards indefinitely reprinted and epitomized. Our

6 *De duplici copia verborum ac rerum,* Leyden ed. T. I. fo. 3-110.

author's *De conscribendis epistolis,* written ten years later (1521) makes more attractive reading, and was very useful, judging from the great number of editions. It is an excellent treatise on the epistolary art by a past-master of the same.[7]

By the side of this treatise upon Latin composition may be placed the polemic *Ciceronianus.*[8] It was a dialogue upon the best form of literary expression, directed against those pedant humanists who recognized Cicero as their only model, and were becoming indecently pagan in thought and expression. The controversy was not new. Intelligent men had fought it out before against the "apes of Cicero." [9] Yet the latter never received a more elaborate drubbing than from this dialogue, in which Erasmus displays his magnificent and enlightened common sense, though at such length as to make a modern reader cry, How long, O Lord!

To us the one side of the argument seems so plain, the opposite so foolish. The Erasmian position, substantially that of Politian, Pico della Mirandola and many others,

[7] Leyden Ed. T. I. fo. 345-484. The excellent Spaniard, Juan Luis Vives (1492-1540), an admirer of Erasmus, merits more than a short note for the excellence and influence of his educational works. He was a man of broad intelligence and moral purpose, an industrious scholar and writer. Living and studying for many years at Louvain, Paris and Bruges, he achieved a cosmopolitan education, while retaining some of his Spanish instincts. He became the educational adviser of Catharine of Aragon and the tutor of the princess Mary. He was more interested than Erasmus in instruction in the vernacular, and equalled him in his intelligent ideas upon juvenile education. His voluminous works have been published, and selections from them translated from the Latin into various languages: into English, for example, by Foster Watson in his *Tudor School-boy Life* (1908) and *Vives and the Renascence Education of Women* (1912). The benevolent intelligence of Vives is strikingly shown in his letter to the Senate of Bruges *Concerning the relief of the Poor, etc.,* translated by Margaret M. Sherwood in *Studies in Social Work,* No. 11 (New York, 1917).

[8] Leyden Ed. T. I. fo. 973-1026, translated by Miss I. Scott, (New York 1908).

[9] Cf. e.g. Vol. I, Chap. 3.

is that Latin still is a living language, to be adapted to present needs, and to the faculties and characters of the living individuals who use it. Cicero also was a living man, as well as a great writer. The whole Cicero, "totus Cicero," is only in himself. Since you are yourself, with your own surroundings, and your own exigencies of conception and expression, you cannot be Cicero, nor think or express yourself through his phrases. In attempting to be his mirror, you make a fool of yourself. We should not strive specifically to imitate Cicero, but to imitate or attain to that true art of oratory and writing, which we find in him, and in others also. Some change of forms, some novelties of expression are demanded by novel subjects and novel thoughts. Christian thoughts, for example, will not altogether fit the language of Cicero. Every phrase, every word, once had its inception. If novelty were always barbarism, every word was once a barbarism.

Erasmus shows all this through the convincing satire of his Dialogue. His own theory and practice recognized the rightfully constraining power of the genius of a language upon everyone using it in speech or writing. Within that broad conformity, there was scope for individual genius to express itself, as it did in fact in his own writings. Theirs was a pure Latinity, a formal Latin grace; yet they were pervaded and enlivened by a personal variety of style adapted to the subject and the situation.

The evil pedantry which eschewed all words and phrases not found in Cicero, had led, argues the Dialogue, to a paganization of Christian concepts in a clasical nomenclature; it was part and parcel of the paganism which was pervading conduct, ethics, religion, till it threatened not merely to color, but to vitiate the Christian life. "We are Christian in name only," says the right-minded interlocutor. The opposite should be striven for; all our studies should have the effect of making us better Christians; they should be pursued to the glory of Christ: "His est totius eruditionis et eloquentiae scopus."

If the last words seem an echo of pious convention,

Erasmus nevertheless believed that all scholarship should make for a better understanding of Christianity. Before tracing the proof of this in his religious writings and sacred studies, let us notice his *Adagia* which were so effective in spreading the humanizing influence of the classics. Like Montaigne after him, he had a genius for modernizing their lessons, and making them live again in the life of the present. In him humane studies produced their perfect fruit in the dissemination of human enlightenment. His whole life was educational for himself and for his age. There was instruction in everything he wrote, in his educational tracts which we have noticed, in his religious writing, in his editings and translations, in his imaginative *Colloquies* and symbolic Satire, and nowhere more diffusely than in his huge volume of *Adagia*.[10]

Most genially this great work adapted the wisdom of the Greeks and Romans to the tempers and understanding of sixteenth century Europeans. It became the commonplace book, *par excellence,* from which everyone, including Luther himself, drew his classical quotations. Year by year, Erasmus enlarged the collection for successive editions, until they became "Thousands four of Adages," as published the year he died. The name included what one would, in the way of proverbs, pithy sayings, admirable phrases, taken from the Ancients. They were all full of vitality, pregnant with meaning, charged with consideration of life.

The scholastic spirit, the need to classify and present through classification, worked in the author while he was writing his prolegomena and was setting forth the many uses of the wisdom packed in these old sayings. Yet their charm and usefulness were but academically suggested by the statement that the knowledge of proverbs conduces to many ends, and most potently to four, to wit: ad philosophiam, ad persuadendum, ad decus et gratiam orationis, ad intelligendos optimos quosque auctores.

10 The *Adages* fill Tome II of the Leyden edition, fo. 1-1212.

Having got the prolegomena off his mind, Erasmus begins auspiciously with pleasant comment on his first proverb, τὰ τῶν φίλων κοινά id est, Amicorum communia sunt omnia. He speaks of the early forms of this thought, and then of its later applications, as among the Romans, and so makes clear its general human value. He usually gives the original Greek saying first, and then its Latin equivalent, with the Greek and then the Latin examples of its use. The first proverb of the "first century" of the "Second thousand" is again an apt instance—"Σπεῦδε βραδέως, i.e., festina lente," and he expands the matter of its wisdom through several folios. The third thousand opens with the Ἡράκλειοι πόνοι, i.e., Herculei labores. This is, as it were, a topic become proverbial, and Erasmus elucidates it with abundant comment, as he does also the more cryptic Sileni Alcibiadis.

Occasionally his treatment of a proverb expands into an essay. A noted instance is the *Dulce bellum inexperto,* which opens the Fourth Thousand, and has been frequently published and translated separately.[11] Erasmus hated war, as well might one whose life had been surrounded by its fruitless ravages. Tellingly he gives the adverse arguments, which applied so obviously to the Franco-Italian-Spanish struggles, with which he was familiar, as he was writing this pacifist tract about the year 1514. His arguments do not quite reach the case of a state or people protecting its freedom from a foreign foe and a domestic tyrant. It is easy to point out the wickedness of dynastic wars, and the folly of Xerxes invading Greece; but the armory of the stoutest pacifist would be taxed to find a valid argument against resistance on the part of the victors of Marathon and Salamis.

The lengthy disquisition is exceptional in the *Adagia,* where the vast majority of proverbs and phrases are treated shortly. In 1532 Erasmus published a not entirely

11 The old English translation is printed—*Erasmus against War* —in the Humanist Library (Boston 1907).

dissimilar work, his eight books of *Apophthegmata,* which were saying and incidents carrying a lesson, collected from the Ancients and adapted to the use of youthful princes. In them the brave Lacedaemonians pass before us, Socrates and the philosophers, Philip of Macedon, his great son, and many other valiant worthies and wise men. Quite pleasantly the lengthy work [12] followed the *Adages* in adapting the experience of the ancients to contemporary needs and tastes.

The religious writings and sacred studies of Erasmus, capped by his edition of the New Testament in Greek, would have been more palpably epoch-making had not the tumultuous genius of Luther merged all things gentler in a vast explosion. In Erasmus the love of letters fed the desire to let the light of reason fall temperately upon the profane and sacred follies of mankind. The same love of letters and of reasonableness held him back from Luther's paths of violence, an abstention destined to embitter his later years.

When about thirty-five years old, his temper still unwarped by controversy, he wrote, nominally for a carnal-minded friend,—the *Enchiridion Militis Christiani.*[13] It was an outline of Erasmian piety, and quickly became a popular manual. The friend, or his godfearing wife, apparently had asked Erasmus to prescribe a "vivendi rationem" or system of living, by which he might attain a mind worthy of Christ. Erasmus's title means either Manual or Dagger of the Christian soldier; and he begins with the assertion that the Christian life is warfare. Rites and professions will not help, unless we fight verily and spiritually against evil. This is the constant Erasmian ethical religious note. The *Enchiridion* will lay stress upon the heart set right and striving valiantly for Christ, and will minimize the value of ceremonies, vows, outward acts, and even the dogmatic theological element. The worthlessness of the outer act,

12 Leyden Ed. T. IV fo. 93-379.
13 Leyden Ed. T. V fo. 1-66. Written in 1501, published in 1503.

when unaccompanied by any change of heart, had been recognized by good men and even by the Church before Erasmus. Yet he perceived this spiritual principle with ethical intelligence. There was a more portentous spiritual originality in his subconscious depreciation of dogmatic theology. Definitude, elaborate exactness of orthodoxy, he made little of. His reason and his humane studies thus led him into what many of his contemporaries deemed rationalism in a bad sense, but to which modernity will attach no evil imputation.

Yet the rationality of Erasmus was not quite freed from its intellectual environment. The second chapter of the *Enchiridion* indicates that he had not disembarrassed himself of the conventional allegorical interpretation of Scripture.[14] He and his fellow humanists of Italy and elsewhere commonly applied the same fancy to the interpretation of the classic poets. "As divine Scripture has little fruit for him who sticks to the letter, so the Homeric and Virgilian poetry will be found helpful if one remembers that it is all allegorical—eam totam esse allegoricam—which none denies whose lips have so much as tasted the learning of the ancients."

Chapter third of the *Enchiridion* had for its topic the wisdom which is self-knowledge, and the distinction between the false knowledge of the world and the true wisdom of Christ which the world thinks folly.[15] A manual of the Christian life could not omit these topics. Hence this chapter and several following, in which with little novelty Erasmus shows man to be *corpus* and *mens:* without the first, he were a deity; without the second he were a swine. There is also the usual teaching concerning the outer and the inner man; and the threefold man, anima, spiritus, carnis, is spoken of with little novel insight. Erasmus does better in his practical applications, for instance

14 See *Enchiridion,* Cap. II and Cap. VIII, Canon V.
15 Fo. 11. Using phrases from Paul, Erasmus here adumbrates some of the meanings which he will attach to this word *stultitia* in his "Praise of Folly."

in pointing out that man may love Christ in his own wife, when he cherishes Christlike qualities in her.

His eighth chapter sets forth, without much novelty, the rules of Christian living: the point is the moral purpose of the act, the end for which it is done. This determines the religious worth of fasting and prayer, of letters and learning, and likewise the worship of the saints. "Deem Christ to be no empty word, but nothing else than love, simplicity, patience, purity; in fine, whatever he taught. Understand the devil to be nothing else than that which draws one from these." Taken by itself this is sheer morality, emptied of dogma. But Erasmus trims the course of his argument to navigate the open sea, if not the tortuous bays, of the accepted faith. He had no fancy to cast down whatever might be upheld with rational decency.

So he continues through this treatise, sensible and intelligent, pointing always to the intent and moral purpose, keeping means distinct from ends; showing how the spiritual life does not lie in observances, but in the love of neighbor; and how monks, even those reputed holy, may walk not in the spirit, but in the very flesh, with fasts and vigils. In this full sense, Christ is the end of the Law; one shall change his heart, rather than his garment; follow the spiritual lesson and imitate the Virgin and the saints, to whom one prays. Erasmus would not sanction reliance on the sacraments, without spiritual conformity to their import. For the still carnal-minded Christian, worship may be no better than the sacrifice of bulls to heathen gods. Yet he does not condemn rites performed as outer manifestations of the spirit, or as an aid to such as need them. He who does not feel this need, should still follow the observances that he may not cause his weaker brother to stumble.[16]

The years 1511 to 1514 were passed by Erasmus

[16] The rational qualities of the *Enchiridion* reappear in the *Institutio Principis Christiana*, written for Charles V. Leyden Ed. T. IV fo. 560-612.

chiefly at Cambridge. During portions of this period he taught Greek grammar and lectured on the Letters of Jerome. But the best of his time seems to have been put upon his forthcoming editions of Jerome's *Opera* and the Greek New Testament, on both of which he had long been working. From Cambridge he proceeeded to Basel to arrange for their publication with Froben. Scholars and printers connected with the great printing-house of Amorbach and Froben were already preparing an edition of Jerome; and Erasmus joined his work to theirs. By 1516 the complete edition appeared. Erasmus gave his time also to editions of Augustine and other Church Fathers. But that spent on Jerome, especially upon his epistles, was a labor of love; for above all the other fathers, he admired Jerome, who, he says in a letter to Leo X, delights by his eloquence, teaches by his erudition, ravishes by his holiness. He is tempted to place Jerome's style above Cicero's; this was rhetorical exaggeration. But the writings of this admirable scholar and letter-writer appealed most sympathetically to Erasmus.

Reasons for going behind the Vulgate to the Greek text of the New Testament appealed to few. For what strikes us as the only sure method, that of always looking beyond popular versions to the original document, was then accepted only by the most advanced scholarship; and when applied to Scripture it seemed subversive of authority and faith. The theology of the early sixteenth century, like that of the fifteenth or the twelfth, in so far as it rested upon Scripture and its interpretation, rested on the Vulgate. To suggest that there was a more certain text might impugn the authority of the Church, not to mention the Holy Ghost who always had inspired the Church's dictates and beliefs.

So one realizes how profoundly educational was the publication of the Greek New Testament, with annotations upon its meanings and a revised Latin version; also what suspicion and disapproval were aroused. An example may be given from the well-meaning pen of his correspondent Dorphius, who sought by expostulation and lengthy argument to turn Erasmus from his undertaking: "You are proposing to correct the Latin copies by the Greek. But if I show you that the Latin version has no mixture of falsehood or mistake, will you not admit that such a work is unnecessary? But this is what I claim for the Vulgate, since it is unreasonable to suppose that the Universal Church has been in error for so many generations in her use of this edition, nor is it probable that so many holy Fathers have been mistaken, who in reliance upon it have defined the most arduous questions in General Councils, which, it is admitted by most theologians as well as lawyers, are not subject to error in matters of faith." [17]

Besides such decent arguments, there was abuse from the more violent. But Erasmus cut the wind from many hostile sails by obtaining the approval of Pope Leo X, and dedicating the work to him. He laid stress upon his reverence and conservatism.

"The New Testament in Greek and Latin," he writes to Leo in August, 1516, "revised by us, together with our annotations, has been published for some time, under the safeguard of your auspicious name. I do not know whether the work pleases everyone, but I find that up to this time, it has certainly been approved by the principal theologians. . . . By this labour we do not intend to tear up the old and commonly accepted edition, but to emend it in some places where it is corrupt, and to make it clear where it is obscure; and this is not by the dreams of my own mind, nor as they say, with unwashed hands, but partly by the evidence of the earliest manuscripts, and partly by the opinion of those whose learning and sanctity have been confirmed by the authority of the Church, I mean Jerome, Hilary, Ambrose, Augustine, Chrysostom, and Cyril. Meantime we are always prepared to give our reasons, without presumption, for anything which we

17 Trans. from Nichols, *Epist. of Erasmus*, II, p. 169.

have rightly taught, or to correct, without grudging, any passage where, as men, we have unwittingly fallen into error." [18]

In the preface to the later edition of 1524, Erasmus says: Habemus fontes Salvatoris—what but salvation can we draw from them? It is safer to go to them than read the theologians. It is proper to draw from the sources this philosophy—hanc philosophiam—from which we are called Christians. Whoever would be called such, should not be ignorant of the *dogmata* of his King. Who could be a Franciscan and not know the *regula* of Francis; so one should know the *regula* of Christ.

For the editing of the text, Erasmus had not the apparatus, or the knowledge, or the painstaking habit of modern scholarship. Yet he perceived the problems and difficulties which he had not the patience and equipment to solve. Incited perhaps by Colet's way of viewing Paul's epistles in their historical setting, Erasmus weighed the human knowledge, or ignorance, possessed by the inspired writers of the New Testament, and sought to elucidate their meanings from a consideration of the historical conditions under which they wrote. He was brave as a scholar. If ingenuousness did not mark his relations with friends and patrons, and if the dilemmas of a distasteful religious conflict drove him to tergiversation, he never lacked courage when defending the freedom of intelligent thinking and the sort of truth he understood and cared for. It was the bravery of a man defending his own home.

Erasmus effectively defended his Greek Testament, as well as his Latin version and his separately published Paraphrase, in an *Apologia Argumentum* "against certain unlearned and evil men." A passage not of a polemic nature may be given to show how he expressed the views of sundry of his mediaeval predecessors in open-

18 Trans. from Nichols o. c. II, p. 316. See also Erasmus to Bullock, Nichols, o. c. II, pp. 324 sqq.

mindedness. More than one of them had found fore-shadowings of Christian truth in the heathen philoso-phers; and it was also a usual conviction, picturesquely set forth by Hugo of St. Victor,[19] that the Old Testament was the *umbra* of the New. Erasmus expresses the same opinions:

"Since the Old Testament was the shadow and pre-paratory discipline for the Evangelical Philosophy, and since the Evangelical teaching is at once the restora-tion and perfection of nature, as first created in purity, it should not seem surprising if it were given to cer-tain gentile philosophers, by the force of nature to dis-cern some matters which agree with the doctrine of Christ. Paul bears witness that, from the visible fabric of the world, they gathered what the eye could not see, but the mind could comprehend, even the eternal power and divinity of God. It was especially congruous that Christ should bring nothing save that of which the shadow or scintilla had gone before in the books of the Old Testament, by which the faith of all would be the more inclined toward a thing not altogether sud-den and unexpected. Therefore, whatever Christ set forth, was first promised in the oracles of the holy prophets, shadowed in figures, and even fragmentarily expressed." [20]

This passage presents the fact of spiritual evolution or development, as many passages had done in the works of mediaeval doctors. But in the Middle Ages, and still in the time of Erasmus, men saw more definitely than today the preordainment of God and his providential direction of the entire process.

Two works remain to be spoken of, perhaps the most constantly read of all Erasmus's writings, both in his life-

19 See *The Mediaeval Mind*, Vol. II, p. 100.
20 Erasmus, *Epistola de Phil. Evangelica*, printed in T. VI of the Leyden Ed. before the New Testament.

time and since his death: The *Praise of Folly* and the *Colloquies*.[21] Though differing in form, they agree in substance; and together express the opinions of the author upon those matters of contemporary life, belief, and superstition, which roused his interest, elicited his approval, or drew his criticism and contempt.

The *Praise of Folly* is called a *declamatio* by its author, a term carrying the idea of something entertaining. That the composition was a jeux d'esprit is abundantly stated in a letter of dedication to Thomas More,[22] in whose house the book was written. Its scheme had been the writer's diversion when returning from Italy; and now he wished the protection of More's name "For wranglers perhaps will not be wanting, who may assail it, on the score that these trifles are sometimes more frivolous than becomes a theologian, and again more biting than accords with Christian moderation; or will exclaim that we are bringing back the Old Comedy or the pen of Lucian, and seizing everything with the teeth." Yet study should have its relaxations, especially when they are such as may bring suggestion to the reader who is not dull. "Others will pass judgment on me; and yet, unless I am egregiously deceived by self-conceit, we have praised Folly not altogether foolishly." It is not too biting, seeing that he has mentioned no names, and has impartially satirized the vices of all sorts and conditions of men.

So then the *Praise of Folly* is a satire, meant to amuse, but also, as gradually becomes evident, intended to instruct and improve. The writer does not bind himself to any single idea of his protagonist. Folly has many shades of meaning. At the first it appears as life's hilarious and

21 Μωρίας Ἐγκώμιον id est *Stultitiae Laus, declamatio*, Leyden Ed. IV fo. 402-504, first published in 1511; *Colloquia familiaria*, Leyden Ed. I, 627-890; first published in 1516, and added to in the innumerable subsequent editions.

22 Printed and usually translated with the work; also by Nichols, *Epist. of Erasmus*, II, p. 1 sqq.

impulsive energy of desire, a child of Plutus.[23] Folly is impulse, childish or mature, innocent or debased, at all events not disillusioned. For illusion is a part of desire and action; who is without it is a dried and hamstrung Stoic!

At first the book makes kindly and approving fun of the ways of action and the foibles and weaknesses of mankind. It is not mordant, only amused. But gradually from fools innocent and natural and undebased, it passes to those whose illusions are vicious in their setting and results. Such are stultified grammarians, scribblers, sophisters; such are passionate dicers; and then those addicted to the marvellous and incredible, gaping fools, greedy of strange tales, who ascribe virtue to shrines and images, and to vows made to saints. Worse than such are they who rely on rotten pardons, and think to measure, as by clepsydras, the ages, years, months, days, which they have knocked off from Purgatory. Priests promote these evil follies, and reap gain from them. Now the satire becomes mordant: it ridicules, it lashes the fool-vices, their panders and their votaries; the fool-sophisters, Scotists, dabblers in split hairs and things incomprehensible, and the like-minded theologians, with their impossible fool-questions; and then the Monks! These are well scourged. As to kings, allowance is made for the blinding effect of their exalted station; but their courtiers are handled roughly. The discourse pounces upon Popes and Cardinals and bishops; the lashing becomes merciless. Luther might lay on more violently, but not more deftly.

After this, the satirical element is genially dispersed; the bitterness is past. Citing first the sayings of gentile authors and then the teaching of Christ, Folly finds the earth full of fools, and none to be called good or wise save God alone. Folly is part of man, and may even be his better part, more excellent than his wisdom. St. Paul

[23] One may compare it with that all-embracing animal desire symbolized by Rabelais in his "Gaster." See Vol. III, Chap. 4.

speaks "as a fool." Christ bids his followers consider the
lilies of the field; bids them take no thought of what
they shall say when delivered up. Woe unto the wise!
he cries, and gives thanks to his Father for having hidden the Kingdom of heaven from them and revealed it
unto babes. Seeing that "the foolishness of God is wiser
than man," let us be "fools for Christ's sake," for the
sake of Him who crowned his life by the "foolishness
of the Cross." In fine, concludes the author, "the Christian religion seems to have some relationship with folly,
and is not in accord with wisdom." The true Christian
will scorn the crowd which relies on the ceremonial of
the flesh, and address himself utterly to the spirit. The
crowd will think this insanity. And truly the life which
is in the spirit and has foretaste of eternal beatitude,
partakes of madness, like the madness of lovers praised
by Plato.

The *Colloquies,* the Familiar Talks or Dialogues, of
Erasmus passed through sixty editions in the author's
life-time. Condemned by the Sorbonne, also denounced
by Luther, they only became more widely read; they were
used in schools as texts of Latinity and of enlightenment.
They had been written and brought together by the author in the course of the twenty-five years or so beginning about 1500. More voluminous, more multifarious,
than the Praise of Folly, they are withal simpler. No elu-
sively doubling thread of meaning runs through them;
they are just what they are, a series of familiar dialogues,
between various fictitious persons, upon almost any topic
of daily life or current practice and opinion. Opening in
formulae of polite conversation; they quickly turn to chat
of plays and pastimes; of horse-cheats and the tricks of
common beggars; of the villainies of a soldier's life; of
the contemptible lots of benefice-hunters; of early rising
and temperate living; of marriages and funerals; of con-
vivial feasts and those at which there is more serious
flow of soul. They discuss common superstitions, rash
vows, and the deceits practised on would-be nuns; the

vain pilgrimages made to St. James of Compostella and across the sea; they hold up to view the heathen follies, the ceremonials and corruptions, which marked the conduct of the Church. The speakers are shown in all manner of situations: in shipwrecks, funerals, on silly pilgrimages, fooled by astrologers and alchemists, grovelling in superstition or practising upon the superstitious. Through them runs the most uncommon common sense of the writer; his intelligent apprehension of the real point; his rational consideration of it. One sees his tolerance of whatever is not positively false and harmful; his respect for honest and respectable opinion, qualities conducing to a recognition of the worth of honest scholarship and the desirableness of intellectual freedom, within the bounds of decency. The book itself is brave and free in its ridicule of abuses which still reposed on the authority of the Church, and from which came part of the Church's revenue.

Erasmus maintained that he attacked the abuse and not the ecclesiastical institution. But attacks on the one are apt to smirch the other. Men do not notice such distinctions. An attack on indulgences goes to the heart of much, although one may insist that nothing has been said against absolution following upon repentance and atonement. Who shall draw the line between abuse and institution? And in Christianity, when has the line been drawn between true faith and piety, and the superstitions wrapping the hearts of ignorant believers? Assuredly the worship of the Virgin and the saints is a Roman Catholic tenet. But "The Shipwreck" [24] ridicules calling on the saints and on the Virgin by flattering titles. What had she to do with the Sea? Note the utterly disintegrating answer: "In ancient times, Venus took care of mariners, because she was believed to be born of the sea; and because she has left off to take care of them, the Virgin Mother was put in the place of her that was a mother,

24 Vol. I, p. 275 sqq. of Bailey's translation, 2 vols. (London, 1878). It is the *Naufragium*, Leyden Ed. I. fo. 712 sqq.

but not a Virgin." This quite indelibly connects the worship of the Virgin with the heathen cult of Venus.

In the *Religious Pilgrimage*,[25] more ridicule is put upon the Virgin and the saints and upon pilgrimages. At the end, the sensible speaker tells how he, who never saw Rome, performs *his* Roman Stations: "After that manner I walk about my house, I go to my study, and take care of my daughter's chastity; thence I go into my shop, and see what my servants are doing; then into the kitchen, and see if anything be amiss there; and so from one place to another, to observe what my wife, and what my children are doing, taking care that everyone is at his business. These are my Roman Stations." Such excellent sense may be rather solvent of religious observance.

But the *Colloquies* give utterance to a piety which is direct, sincere, ethical, pregnant with the religion of the spirit. Examples are "An Enquiry concerning Faith," "The Religious Treat," and "A Child's Piety." [26] In the last the excellent youth, stating his own creed, comes near to stating that of Erasmus: "I believe firmly what I read in the Holy Scriptures, and the Creed called the Apostles, and I don't trouble my head any farther; I leave the rest to be disputed and defined by the clergy, if they please; and if anything is in common use with Christians that is not repugnant to the Holy Scriptures, I observe it for this reason, that I may not offend other people."

His friend asks, "What Thales taught you that philosophy?"

"When I was a boy, and very young, I happened to live in the house of that honestest of men, John Colet."

In this way Erasmus testifies to the pious and reasonable influence exerted on him by that balanced and penetrating English mind.

The purposes, the opinions, the qualities of Erasmus

25 Bailey, o. c. II, 1; Leyden Ed., fo. 774 sqq.
26 This is the *Confabulatio pia*, Leyden Ed. fo. 648 sqq. The two former are fo. 728 sqq.; and 672 sqq. They are all in Vol. I of Bailey's Trans.

reveal themselves in his works. These reflect his environment and his nature, making a very adequate self-expression of the man Erasmus; and the self-expression of a man is always true. Had Erasmus possessed the Titan nature of a Luther, convulsed with convictions as violent as they were trenchant, his self-expression would have appealed to us more pointedly than it does from out the compass of those huge ten folios of the Leyden edition. His innumerable writings did their work in their time, and still interest us historically. They spread the Erasmian personality before us. He who may bring himself to read them will note everywhere facility of presentation, broad, proportioning scholarship, not too exact, nor always profound; balanced common sense and clear intelligence which grasp the veritable point; interest in well authenticated fact, linguistic, historical and rational, which is the scholar's truth; care for what is truly ethical, dependent on motive and interest, and not bound up in ceremony and observance; insistence on unhampered study, on the rights of scholarship, on freedom to reach the most rationally verified result; recognition also of mutually tolerating differences of sensible opinion, but no patience for wilful ignorance and stubbornness; a cherishing of piety and rational religion, but with no taste for dogma or metaphysics, and as little for the transports of religious rapture.

Erasmus followed earthly, rather than heavenly light. He cared for the religion of Christ, and he loved scholarship. From some of his expressions one or the other might seem his chief care. But, with him, both belonged to the same quest of rational truth. He followed letters; as a scholar also he studied Scripture, still seeking to establish the surest record of the Faith. He was the scholar, not the sceptic, in religion; and never doubted of the salvation brought by Christ, as evidenced by Scripture. Thus he was evangelical, but tolerantly, without a wish to tear down whatever had been recognized or built up by the Church, so far as it did not counter either the Gospel or a rational morality.

One can foresce the attitude of such a nature toward the Lutheran Reformation. As was generally said, no one had done as much to open men's eyes to the follies, abuses and corruptions, infecting the Roman Catholic religion. His writings had had universal currency and corresponding influence. The number of editions printed of them one and all is almost incredible.[27] Never was a scholar so widely read; and never was a scholar's word more potent. It seems safe to say that no man had done as much to prepare the mind of Europe for religious reformation as Erasmus of Rotterdam [28]

Yet when it came through Luther, he could not go along with it. It was to be national; this universal Latinist had no appreciation of nationality. It was to be passionate, violent, intolerant, proceeding with fixed ideas. There was little here to gain his sympathy. Still less could he sympathize with the Catholic Church, which was more corrupt and quite as violent. With his mind set on enlightened scholarship, both sacred and profane, how could Erasmus not oppose whatever threatened either? How he hated this mutual intolerance and wrath, which might extinguish letters and intellectual freedom!

There had been a conflict into which he could throw himself with all his mind, because there, as it seemed to him, one side stood for piety and the full light of scholarship, while the other's strength lay in ignorance and prejudice. It was the struggle of Johann Reuchlin, against those who fought to suppress the study of Hebrew and with it the freedom of letters. Erasmus was on Reuchlin's

27 The stupendous lists are modestly and succinctly given in *Biblioteca Erasmiana, Repertoire des oeuvres d'Erasme,* published in 1893 at Ghent, and distributed gratis and graciously to promote the study of Erasmus.

28 By the year 1517, Erasmus's religious influence had been recognized: "me Christum sapere docuisti," ("You have taught me to know Christ.") writes one correspondent, Allen o. c. II; p. 341 (1516), and another hails him: "Salve Erasme vas electionis et secunde post Paulum doctor gentium." ("Hail to thee, Erasmus, vessel of the Word and second only to Saint Paul as the teacher of nations.") Allen o. c. II, p. 505.

side. He felt himself defending everything he cherished, while Reuchlin's persecutors were the kind of men he detested and despised.[29]

Erasmus's later years were made unhappy by the parting of the ways between the humanism of the North and the Reform which at first it had seemed to carry in its train. He recognized no hostile rivalry between secular and religious truth. It was monstrous that the truth which came by faith should not respect the aid of letters and cherish the truth which came through scholarship. Toward the end he wrote bitterly to Pirckheimer: "Wherever Lutheranism reigns, there is an end to letters. Yet these men have been chiefly (maxime) nourished on letters." [30] His life had been an unhampered progress in scholarship and fame till the Lutheran controversy reached such importance as to compel men to take sides. Incapable of this, Erasmus became suspect to both and was driven to subterfuge. His discomfort and unhappiness appear in his correspondence from this time to the close of his life.[31]

Erasmus never could have joined with Luther. The opposite tempers of the two would have held them apart. And before many years, Erasmus thought he saw the Reform throwing the world into a spiritual and political anarchy. But he could not go along with the Church in its measures to suppress the Reform; for he detested persecution, and deemed force worse than useless in matters of the Faith. The Church should conquer only through its reasonableness and its persuasion, and its imitation of Christ. Alas! neither side seemed to hold a brief for scholarship and the simple truth and freedom of the

[29] See Nichols, *Epist. of Erasmus*, Vol. II, pp. 189, 193, and ante, Chapter VI. Later, under stress of the Lutheran conflict, Erasmus was inclined to minimize his interest in Reuchlin. See Ep. to Wolsey (1519), Allen, o. c. III, p. 589.

[30] Leyden Ed. T. III, Ep. 1006, fo. 1139.

[31] The letter to Wolsey, 1519, Allen o. c. III, p. 587 sqq., is typical. See ib. III, pp. 527 and 540.

Gospel. In the end, Erasmus elected to adhere to the Church; and it was as touching the point of veritable freedom, free-will indeed, on which he first formally took his stand against the teaching of Luther. His *de libero Arbitrio* (1524) evinced his common sense in the matter and showed him on the side of freedom, to which he felt free-will to be essential.

At all events he was *facile princeps* among the men of letters of the North. He enumerates his works in the *Catalogus* addressed to Botzheim in 1523.[32] Touching upon reflections made upon him by Luther's friends, he says:

"they have nothing that they can bring against me, except that I would not profess at the peril of my head, what either I did not accept, or held as doubtful, or did not approve, or should have professed to no purpose. For the rest, who has written more against faith in ceremonies, against the superstition of fasts, of cult and vows, against those who ascribe more to the commentaries of men than to the divine Scriptures, who set human edicts above God's precepts, and rely for aid upon the saints more than on Christ himself; against the scholastic theology corrupted by philosophic and sophistic subtleties, against the rashness of defining what you will; against the absured opinions of the crowd? . . . These and much besides, which I have taught according to the measure of grace given me, I have taught steadfastly, not clamoring against anyone who could teach something better. And Erasmus has taught nothing but rhetoric (eloquentiam)! Would that they could persuade my silly friends of this, who continually boast that whatever Luther has taught he has drawn from my writings! . . . The sum of my crimes is that

32 Allen, o. c. I, pp. 1-46. The passage I have translated is on p. 29. Compare it with the letter to Gacchus, Leyden Ed. T. III, col. 1724-1730.

I am more moderate; and for this I hear ill things from both sides, because I exhort both to gentler counsels. I do not condemn liberty founded on love."

Erasmus was not always quite so sweet as in the last phrase.

Chapter 3

The Spiritual and Political Preparation for Luther

IF EVER A MAN EXPRESSED HIMSELF and his people, it was Martin Luther. Yet he spoke mainly in the language of the past. His doctrines won their acceptance through their religious strength, their timely pertinency to the German social and political situation, and through their emphatic statement. Luther's power of expression drove his teachings into the German mind. The rugged phrases of the *Address to the German Nobility* and *The Freedom of the Christian man* worked themselves into the German blood. Yet still they spoke in the language of the past. If Luther violently rejected such of its formularies as shocked his intelligence and countered his convictions, he continued to express himself and his people through old and well-tried forms. But he brought to his expression his own spiritul experiences and his understanding of the world about him.

Expression in language is not merely the symbol of thought, but its completion, its finished form. Sometimes, however, as these symbols, these phrases or formulations, pass from one generation to another, they fall out of accord with other thoughts and convictions, fruits of further experience and knowledge, which may be seeking expression in the later time. To some more zealously advancing minds, old symbols and formulations will seem to have become outworn, used up, fit only for discarding and the new time's intellectual scrap-heap; and even more patient souls may dumbly feel that their time-honored thoughts fail to bring comfort or conviction. In fine as the old symbols cease to correspond with the current consideration of life, they cease to express vitally the later generation.

Moreover, when concepts or symbols, and the institutions in which they may have been incorporated, cease to correspond with the thinking of a later time, and for that reason are no longer instinct with life, then, like sickly human bodies, they become open to corruption, prone to disease. This is seen most clearly when the conception has worked itself out in customs, pilgrimages for example, or the granting of indulgences for sins; or when it is embodied in an institution, monasticism, if one will, or a priesthood, or a universal church. Let us note some incidents of the course through which concepts or symbols conceived in the patristic period, or before it, and accepted in the Middle Ages, were developed into dogmas, expanded in beliefs, and incorporated in institutions. Then how some of them began to lose their validity, and became husks.

The Gospel symbolized divine strength, virtue, love, in the life and words and acts, the personality in fine, of Christ. The vitality of that symbol Christ has not passed away, because it has not ceased to correspond with human thoughts and yearnings. But in the centuries following the Crucifixion, Christ was elaborated, sublimated, rendered metaphysical in dogma, fixed in the larger symbol of the Trinity. This formulation obliterated some of the qualities which had been very living in the Gospel Christ. Thereupon the needy human mind, as it were, out of the lost bits of Christ, made other symbols. Chief among them was the Virgin Mary, symbol of refuge, preserving the divine qualities of love and pity and forgiveness that they might not be entombed in the metaphysics of the Triune God. Mary and the saints and angels were symbols made by the plastic mind in answer to its longings; symbols of realized assurance, they were held in the imagination, seen in visions, even touched in states of rapture. Yet with all their loveliness and comfort, they tended to lose vitality as the sixteenth century approached. For they no longer corresponded with men's larger thoughts of the workings of the divine. They had even taken on corruption, in that they had been brought to pander to what the keener moral perceptions of the time recognized as immoralities.[1] Soon they would be numbered among superstitions by large sections of Europe.

Monasticism was the expression of another Christian ideal. The celibate ascetic life for men and women represented the fear of the devil, the horror of sin, the anxious detestation of the world and the flesh; also a yearning for purity, utter devotion to the Crucified. Through monastic living and mortification of the flesh, and abject penitence, ardent men and women had reached assurance and consolation, even had attained to union with God. Monasticism had had a great rôle in Christianity; had been instituted and developed, had fallen from its high estate, and had been time and again reformed. Its reformers and reinstitutors—Benedict, Damiani, Bernard, Gulgo, Francis,—presented phases of its ideals: their lives also had become symbols. There was abundant monastic slackness and corruption in the sixteenth century. If that had resulted from the sheer weakness of human nature unable to adhere to an ideal, it might have been remedied again by strenuous reformers. But now monasticism was countered by a new ideal of living. Not human weakness, but a new and rationally supported attitude toward religion and toward life opposed its principles and prepared to demonstrate their invalidity. If the monastic ideal could not keep its throne in the human mind, its practice might become hypocrisy and its pretensions be laughed out of court. That also came to pass in parts of Europe.

The faith of Christ was dogmatized in creeds; first in the simple Apostolic creed, and then in the Nicene elaboration. Both creeds were symbols, the first representing

[1] See, for example, the *Colloquies* of Erasmus, passim, Chap. 2.

the youthful still impressionable body of Christian belief;
the second presenting its rock-ribbed metaphysical conciliar formulation. The Nicene symbol became the citadel
of dogmatic Christianity, with subsidiary dogmas support-
ing it as buttresses. The power of patristic Christian
thought had built it. Through the Middle Ages it stood
sublime, intact, the Faith's foregone conclusion. To bul-
wark this citadel was the chief end of scholastic philosophy. In the fifteenth century the citadel showed no open
signs of weakening. In the sixteenth, Protestants as well
as Catholics professed to lock themselves within it. Yet
it had long stood peak-like above Christian emotion, and
now no longer held or symbolized the vital currents of
Christian thinking. The religious storm swept by it, apparently.

Yet the storm shattered the transubstantiation of bread
and wine, one sacramental buttress, and even disturbed
the "real presence" in the Eucharist. Such dogmas were
not yet emptied symbols, and were fiercely maintained
and contested.

There was a paramount symbol of the unity and to-
tality of the Christian salvation, which the storm con-
spicuously struck, and broke in twain. That was the imperial Roman Catholic Church, visible, tangible, august;
sacerdotal mediator between God and men; sole vehicle
and ministrant of salvation. Not that the thought, the
symbol itself, seemed to have weakened or to have ceased
to correspond with living ideals. Indeed the shattered
reality continued to furnish an ideal to those men who
in fact had broken it. Lutherans and Calvinists professed
to belong to the one true Church composed of all true
believers.

But the concept of the Church had never been quite
settled and at one with itself. At any given moment, it
had a different form in different minds, and it was always
changing. The papal Curia and its priestly supporters did
not hold the same idea as the laity, who paid church
tithes throughout the world, and the secular rulers who
might be hostile to the pope. Unlike the symbol of the

Trinity or that of the Virgin birth, the Church idea was inextricably involved in practice and politics, bound up in things temporal, in the world, the flesh, and the devil. The Church was flesh as well as spirit. Its other-worldly functions might not have been contested, had they not needed to support themselves on temporal power and material emoluments. The concept of the Church had necessarily to embody itself in an institution; and institutions are of this world, part of its dragging needs and lowering practices.

In its temporal and material flesh the Church never could be free from shortcoming and corruption; or fail to be involved in practices inconsistent with its otherworldly purpose. Hence it never could be void of offense; and would always be attacked by saints as well as sinners.

Moreover, its material corruptions were always lowering its doctrines to correspond with its practices, and despiritualizing its teachings. Doubtless, even from Apostolic times unspiritual superstitions had been accepted, like the notion, for example, that the physical thing, the relic or the bread blessed by the priest, might have a magic or miraculous effect, in no way germane to its actual properties. Priests and laity could free themselves from such ideas only by perceiving more clearly that a thing cannot produce something else of an entirely different nature. Cause and effect must lie in the same categories: a physical thing cannot work spiritual miracles; a corporeal act cannot in itself produce a higher spiritual state. Both Erasmus and Luther (not to mention Wyclif) perceived this as touching gifts and pilgrimages and mortifications of the flesh. Possibly some such rational principle might before their time have been accepted by the Church, had not the needs of the Church as a temporal institution proved an obstacle. Instead, irrational unspiritual notions, which may have had their root in paganism, were retained through this degrading influence, and sometimes were aggravated. It was the plainly corrupt and material abuse of these derelict notions that aroused men's indignation; otherwise the doctrines themselves would have quietly fallen away or remained as negligible anachronisms. Luther's attack upon Indulgences and its immense results afford the most obvious illustration, while the futility of the reforming purposes of Erasmus was partly due to their primarily intellectual character. They demonstrated the absurdity of prevalent irrationalities in doctrines and practices, instead of attacking directly the corruptions which made those irrationalities abominable, and were the real reasons for overthrowing them. His labors helped to prepare men's minds. The explosion came otherwise.

The preparation for the revolt of Luther from the Roman Catholic Church is not to be sought in specific antecedents which happen to agree in form with some of the reformer's thoughts. Such merely mark the milestones on the way. Luther's revolt was led up to by the intellectual, economic and political progress of Europe and, especially, of the German people. As the mentality of Europe advanced in the fourteenth and fifteenth centuries, disturbing glances were directed toward the Church and the kinds of salvation which it furnished. The differences between peoples became more marked, and the consciousness of nationality stronger. Europe was progressing from homogeneity to diversity. One form of Christianity, one Catholic Church, possibly might no longer answer the spiritual and economic needs of all the nations. At all events, the deepening of the national consciousness of Englishmen and Germans carried some distrust of a church seemingly rooted in an Italian papacy which was always draining other peoples of their gold. Such conditions moved the revolt of Wyclif and led to the Hussite wars.

Religiously the Lutheran revolt and reformation was an announcement of man's dependence upon God for his salvation, to the necessary exclusion of sacerdotal mediation: intellectually it implied insistence upon a revised kind of mental freedom; politically it broke the unity of ecclesiastical authority.

The Church was the Catholic exponent of Christianity.

Luther issued from the Church. Doctrinally, he shook himself free only just so far as he was compelled to by the need to establish his salvation immediately in Jesus Christ. Catholic church doctrine was exceedingly inclusive; suited, in its various aspects or phases to different minds and different tempers. It was an *omnium gatherum* of saving means and doctrines. Luther's rejection of certain of its teachings was grounded in his more absolute acceptance of what it also taught. Salvation by faith had always been proclaimed; yet the Church, as a Catholic result of centuries of accretion, proffered other means of grace for such as needed other disciplines. There were different kinds of Christianity or quasi-Christianity within the Church, with opportunities for religious conviction and practices ranging from the sublime to the abject. Luther, more intense, more consistent, more individual, and more narrow, committed himself to certain Christian doctrines so absolutely and exclusively that others were thereby rejected, many of them make-shift teachings and practices which human weakness demanded, and the Catholic nature of the Church not only tolerated but, as it were, personally felt the need of.

Before Luther, there were men who accepted the same vital doctrines in such a way as to lead them also to reject much that he rejected. There was one Johann von Goch, a Low German or Netherlander, who died in 1475, having made little stir, and leaving writings which were not read by Luther, but were unearthed in later times. Goch held with inchoate pre-Lutheran insistence, upon certain of the doctrines which the Church so catholicly gathered together, along with some ill-sorted practices. He emphasized justification by faith, and held that the Faith should be based upon Scripture, and that the Sacrament did not save when taken by the unrepentant. He also held that the Church might err, which the church knew well enough, but could not formally admit. Another Johann, Joannes de Vesalia, or Wesel, wrote against the papal indulgences issued at the pope's Jubilee of 1450. He maintained that the pope could not absolve from divine punishment, and other things besides, which Luther was to hold.

A more notable figure is still another Johann, this time a Johann Wessel spelled with double s, and if possible not to be confused with his older contemporary, Wesel. Wessel, who lived from 1420 to 1490, had been taught by Thomas à Kempis, his senior by forty years, and is even thought to have influenced his teacher. He early inclined toward Plato, and may have known a little Greek. He studied for many years in Paris, and spent some time in Rome. When sixty years old, he settled down at Heidelberg three years before Luther was born.

Wessel held so many of the doctrines which Luther was to hold, that the latter's enemies reproached him with wholesale borrowing. Luther recognized him as a forerunner, and Erasmus also spoke well of him. He sought to base his theology directly on the Bible, and endeavored to hold to the real meaning of its words. He stated the principle of justification by faith alone, and developed the idea of faith as the source of man's communion with God. Then he followed St. John in the conception of *love,* of God's love of man and man's answering love of God. Love nourishes love, and without it there is no life. Love is perfected in us through the spirit of God, till we are brought where man and angel pass away, and we become a new creature in Christ. The Church is the communion of all the Saints, living and dead. Its bond is love. We have faith in the Gospel through God; and faith in the Church through the Gospel. The reverse is untrue.

Wessel approaches Luther's conception of the priesthood. For him the pope is not infallible; his headship is an accident. The saving effect of the Sacrament depends on the spiritual state of the recipient. Wessel's conception of the Eucharist was less conservative than Luther's; it was like that of Zwingli, and appears to have influenced the radical Carlstadt. He questioned the Catholic doctrines of penance and priestly remission of sins. Christ did not entrust the power to remit sins to any one person, but to the *unity.*—"non uni sed unitati donavit."

The pope cannot exclude man from the grace and love of God, nor enhance the believer's spiritual benefits. Wessel argued against indulgences, advancing, as it were, from the position of Wesel even beyond the points taken by Luther's Theses. Consistently with these ideas, he treats Purgatory as a stage of purification midway between human sinfulness and heavenly perfection. The purgatorial fire is spiritual; it is God himself, and Christ and the Gospel, working in love—an element not absent from Dante's Purgatory.[2]

In spite of the correspondence of their thoughts with Luther's own, these men affected him less than certain contemplative pietists, mystics as they commonly are called, whose ways of thinking were part of Luther's very German religious nature. They also were Germans or Lowlanders by birth. Meister Eckhart was the most creative genius among them, indeed, the creative type of much that was German and of much that became Luther. For this reason a few pages must be devoted to his profound obscurity.

Mysticism is a vague name for much that is amorphous. Along the Rhine and in the Low Countries, a directly yearning and contemplative piety had marked the Brothers of the Free Spirit and the partly kindred evangelical Beghards and Beguines, societies of men and women who had never been high in the Church's favor and were eventually to be treated as heretics. But Mary of Ognies, Elizabeth of Schönau, Hildegarde of Bingen, had been saints of the Church in the twelfth century, and, in the next, with Mechthilde of Magdeburg, the religious impulse had become a personally addressed symbolic and sense passion.[3] In their religious experience there had been scant admixture of justifying reason; but warm had been their zeal for the honor of God and for the purification of His Church. Then had come Meister Eckhart,

---

[2] On Wessel, see Ullmann, *Reformatoren vor der Reformation*, II, pp. 486-514 (Gotha, 1866).

[3] See *The Mediaeval Mind*, Chapter XX.

who was born in Thuringia in 1260 and died in 1327.[4]
His learning and genius made a frame for his religious
impulses, and brought the difficult content of his thought
to striking expression in vital paradox and symbolism.

He was a Dominican and held high office in his Order.
He was likewise a Doctor of Theology, versed in the
teachings of Aquinas, and in the writings of the Arab
commentators of Aristotle. He also had studied Augustine, but seemingly knew best of all the pseudo-Dionysius,
the "Areopagite." There can be no doubt of Eckhart's
full scholastic equipment, which is evinced by his Latin
treatises and to a less degree by his German utterances.

These sermons and other German tracts of Eckhart
disclose a vigorous ethical nature and tense thought, which
they must also have demanded of their auditors. The
Master was a severe thinker. Further, he was a specula-
tive spirit, whose whole being drew toward God, one
might even say toward the ultimate universal reality.
Rather than a scholastic, he was a masterful personality
moulding what he had received into what he was and
would be and attain to. Wherein lay the chief emphasis
of his thought and mood may not be easy for other men
to state.

At all events Eckhart's teaching had to do with God
and the Soul, or with the ultimate reality whereinsoever
that be found. One may also be sure that its rational
structure was but a vehicle of the man's desire and intent, at least if allowance be made for the necessary
attachment of a Dominican Doctor to the scholasticism
represented by his Order. Shall we say, the goal both of
desire and of the thought which justifies it is the soul's
oneness with God? The soul is of the divine essence;
may the completed soul, conscious of its nature and over-
nature, so perfect this union as to convert the Divine
from object to an inner experience? Even God brings his
being to its full actuality and consciousness through com-

4 On Eckhart, see Delacroix, *Mysticisme speculatif en Alle-
magne au 14-siècle* (Paris, 1900).

ing to expression in the beings He creates and remains the essence of. Conversely, the true life of the soul lies in its turning, or perhaps returning, utterly to God, abandoning its worse than worthless distractions, comforts, pleasures. It may profitably exercise this ascetic rejection and mortal humiliation in order to attain its true homing in That which is its source and final blessedness. God, by passing out into His veriest actuality, becomes the true reality of that which He creates; and by knowing this, and living in accord with it, the human creature helps God to fulfil His realization of Himself, till God be All in All. In this perfected absorption which is re-absorption, the Soul attains its heights of love and inner contemplation, which is its bliss and its salvation.

Of this, Christ was and is the absolute example and realization.

"Says our Lord, 'I am gone forth from the Father and am come into the world. Again I leave the world and return to the Father.' Here he means that his coming forth is his entry into the soul. But the soul's entry is her coming forth; she must pass out of her outermost into her innermost, out of her own into the Son's own. Thereupon she is drawn into the Father as the Son leaves the world and returns to the Father with the Soul." But the Son is God, and his coming forth is very God: "His coming forth is his entry. Even as he comes forth from the Father, in the same way he enters the Soul. *His coming forth is God Himself.*" [5]

So creation is God's pouring forth of Himself. This is the old *Emanatio* of Gnostic and Neo-platonist, dear forever to the German mind. One may try to follow Eckhart as he brings similar thoughts to expression in another discourse—on seeing and contemplating God through the "wurckende vernunft," creative reason, the νοὺς ποιητικός

[5] From a sermon on John XVI, 28 (Pfeiffer, *Deutsche Mystiker*, 2, 181. Printed in Vetter, *Lehrhafte Litteratur des 14 u. 15 Jahrhundert*, p. 159).

of the "Areopagite" and of Aristotle, too. "King David said, Lord in thy light shall we see light. . . . Man has within him a light, that is the creative reason; in this light shall he see God in blessedness. Man is created so imperfect that he cannot through his nature know God as creator and as type and form. For this a power above his nature is needed, the light of grace. Now mark my meaning. Saint Paul says, through the grace of God I am that I am. He does not say that he exists through grace. The difference is between being by grace and being [the true] self by grace. The masters says that true form gives being to matter. Now there is much talk among them as to what grace is. I say that grace is nothing else than a light flowing [6] immediately out of the nature of God into the Soul, and it is an over-natural form of the soul that gives it an over-natural being." [7]

So grace imparts a being to the soul exceeding the soul's nature. Without it the soul cannot, beyond her own nature, understand and love. "When the soul is steadfast in an overcoming of herself and passes into a not-herself [8] then is she through grace. . . . This is the highest office of grace that it brings the soul to the true self (das sie die sele bringet in das sie selb [not *ir*-selb] ist). Grace robs the soul of her own works (ir eygen werck), grace robs the soul of her own existence. . . ."

"The worthy Dionysius [the "Areopagite"] says: 'when God is not in the soul, the eternal image is not in the soul, which is her eternal source,' " God keeps this eternal image in the soul through his grace, or light, or "wurck-ende vernunft." In this the soul is raised out of her natural being, which had kept her subject to her own desires that draw away from God. And in this transform-

---

6 With Eckhart's "ein fliessendes liecht," we are back with Mechthilde of Magdeburg and her "fliessendes liecht der Gottheit" —see *The Mediaeval Mind,* Chap. XX.

7 Observe how Eckhart uses the concepts of the dominant Aristotelianism of his Order.

8 . . . stet in einem uberschwang ir selbers und in ein nicht ir selbers geit. . . .

ing of the soul, God is very God: "In my eternal *bild* is God God." [9]

The structural thought of German mysticism is due to Eckhart. As has been often said, this German mysticism was a very inward business. It was a power within each man and woman which might exert itself individually and Germanically, in the end most separatistically, one may say. One seems also to perceive in this German mysticism, as in other things Germanic, the absence of the original discipline, subjection, if one will, to form and order, which the Roman domination imposed upon the peoples of the "Latin" countries.

Eckhart was followed by Ruysbroeck, Suso, Tauler, excellent contemplators all, diffusers and preachers of his thoughts. There is no need to investigate Luther's particular indebtedness to each; for the thoughts of one and all seem to converge in a small pregnant volume, composed toward the close of the fourteenth century, which Luther published and named *Theologia Deutsch*.[10] Deutsch it was unquestionably, and adapted altogether to the German temperament, and not to French reformers, who never liked it. Luther said in his preface that he had not learned more about God, Christ, man and all things, from any other book except the Bible and St. Augustine. *Theologia Deutsch* at all events discloses the contemplative religious elements directly entering the German Reformation.

It opens with Paul's "when that which is perfect is come, that which is in part shall be done away." The perfect is God; the "in part" (geteilte) is the self, the creature; and the perfect comes as the creature puts itself away. Sin is nothing else than the turning of the creature

9 The above is translated from the "Traktat von dem Schauen Gottes durch die wirkende Vernunft" in H. Hildebrand's *Didaktik aus der Zeit der Kreuzzüge*, pp. 38 sqq. (*Deutsche Nat. Lit.*).

10 Luther found the book in 1516, and published it; but gave it this name only in his completed edition of 1518. It has frequently been edited. I have used the edition of Mandel, in *Quellenschriften zur Ges. des Protestantismus* (Leipzig 1908).

from the unchanging good to the changeable, that is, to the imperfect and "in part," and worst of all to itself. This is what the devil did when he would be something. Adam's fall was a turning from God.

How shall there be a restoration? Man can do nothing without God, and God would do nothing without man. So God took on manhood and was made man, and man thereby was made divine (vergottet). Hence I, that is, each one of us, can do nothing without God, and God will do nothing without me. God must be made man (vermenscht) in me, so that He may take on himself all that is in me, until there is nothing of me left that strives against Him. The Incarnation would not help me unless God became man in me. All good and righteousness, yea God himself, cannot help me while remaining without my soul. Eternal blessedness lies in our own soul alone.[11]

And in this renewal and bettering of myself, I do nothing but suffer it to be done. God works it all; I merely suffer His will to be done in me. I hinder God by willing what is me and mine. Yet we do not become loveless, will-less, and without knowledge or perception. Rather these faculties in us become divine, and part of the eternal will and knowledge. The more we make surrender of them, the more perfect they become in us. As Christ's soul went into hell before rising to heaven, so must the soul of man. By realizing its own vileness, it makes the more complete surrender to God.

There is purification, by repentance and renunciation; there is enlightenment, and then union with God. If one could renounce oneself and perfectly obey, he would be free from sin as Christ was. Man is good, better, or best, or the reverse, as he is obedient or disobedient. So the more there is of self-ness and me-ness, the more sin; and the less of me, the more of God.[12]

---

[11] I have changed the position of the last sentence. These and the following passages have much that became part of Luther. One recalls that in the old pagan Mysteries the votary becomes one with the god.

[12] Here Luther wrote on the margin: Quanto decrescit ego

Further on it is said: "Let no one think he can attain true knowledge, or reach the life of Christ, through many questions, or by hearing or reading or study; nor through great skill and cunning, nor through the highest natural reason." Follow Christ in poorness and meekness of spirit. In the union of God, the inner man abides moveless, while the outer man may be tossed hither and thither.[13]

Our extracts have brought us to the middle of the book, which here enters upon a metaphysical discussion of the Absolute Godhead and the conscious working God, recalling the metaphysical side of Eckhart. After beating this upper air for a while, the *Theologia Deutsch* returns to our level with the statement that God does not compel anyone to do or refrain, but suffers each man to act after his will, be it good or bad. God will withstand no one, as Christ bade Peter put up his sword. "Moreover one shall note that God's commands and His enlightenment are addressed to the inner man united with God. And when that takes place, the outer man is taught and directed by the inner man, and needs no outer law or teaching."

The book lays stress upon the distinction, dear to these German contemplators, between the two lights, the false and the true, the divine and the natural.

"The true light is God or divine, the false light is nature or natural. It belongs to God to be neither this or that, nor to will this or that, nor to seek what is particular and individual in the man that is made divine, but only the good as such. So it is with the true light. But it pertains to the creature and to nature to be something particular, and to signify and desire this and that, and not simply to desire what is good, and desire it for the sake of the good, but for the sake of something that is this or that. And as God and the true light are without me-ness and self-ness, and seek not their own, so what

hominis, tanto crescit in eis Ego divinum. (As the man in me shrivels, so waxes the divine spirit in me.)

[13] These sentences, as most of the rest when not in quotation marks, are condensed, rather than literally translated.

is me and mine, and seeks itself and its own in all things, rather than the good as good, belongs to nature and to the false natural light."

It is false, and belongs to the false light, for man to think to be as the Godhead, unmoved, suffering nothing and possessing all. He must not think to transcend the *incarnate* life of Christ on earth. So it pertains to the false light to lift human action above the sphere of the moral conscience, and think whatever it may do is well. The false light curses everything that goes against nature and is hard for man to do. "In fine, where the true light is, there is a true and righteous life, that is pleasing and dear to God. And if it is not the Christlife utterly, it still is patterned on the Christlife and holds it dear. To the Christlife belong honesty, order and all the virtues; it seeks not its own, but only the good, and for goodness's sake. But where the false light is, man is careless of Christ and all the virtues, and cares only for what is pleasing to nature." The false light loves to know too much and too many things, and glories in its knowledge.

So one shall not love himself, but the good. Even God does not love himself as self, and would have greater love for something better, did it exist. All self-love and self-will is sin. He who knows the Christlife, knows Christ; he believes in Christ who believes his life is the best; so much of the Christlife as there is in man, so much Christ is in him. Where the Christlife is, there is Christ; and where it is not, Christ is not.

Reason and will are the noblest in man; but let him know that they are not from himself. The eternal will in its origin and essence is in God; moveless and unworking in Him, it works and wills in the creature's created will. Let the creature not will as of himself, but as if his will were part of God's will. The devil came and Adam, who is nature, and sought to turn the divine will in man into self-will. The noble freedom of the will is to work as God's will; whatever makes it self-will, robs it of this noble freedom. And the freer the will is in this divine freedom, the more repugnant is evil to it, as it was utterly repugnant to Christ. In the Kingdom of heaven, there is no *own;* and anyone there seeking his own would go to hell, and anyone in hell who is without self-will rises to heaven. Man on earth is between heaven and hell, and may turn to the one or the other. By giving up self-will, one comes to Christ, and through Christ to the Father, that is, to the perfect single Good which is all in all, and in which there is no creaturehood or this and that. Disclosure of the perfect good draws the soul to it; and thus the Father draws men to Christ. And no one comes to the Father save through Christ, which is through his life, as has been shown. Thus more than once the book brings human life and thinking back to Christ and to the Christ pattern.

The *Theologia Deutsch* contains much that passed into Luther, much also that devout souls have clung to even to our day. It says nothing about indulgences, or popes or the sacerdotal functions of the priesthood. Yet it annihilated them all. For it presented a religion in which they had no place.

The greatest of all Luther's forerunners, John Wyclif, has not yet been mentioned. He was universally recognized as an arch-heretic, which he certainly was from any Roman Catholic point of view. There is no reason to suppose that Luther read any of his writings, either in the formative period preceding the posting of the Theses against Indulgences or afterwards. John Huss, however, drew his doctrines from the Englishman. Luther appears to have read nothing of Huss, likewise a universally recognized heretic, before the time of his Leipzig disputation with Eck, in the summer of 1519, when he was accused of holding certain views of that schismatical and heretical Bohemian. Soon afterwards he received warm letters from Bohemia, with a book written by Huss; [14] and not long after he declared in an argumentative letter to Eck, that he found himself holding more tenets of Huss than he had

[14] Letter to Staupitz, Oct., 1530, De Wette's edition of Luther's letters, I. p. 341.

held to at Leipzig.[15] Indeed he had "unconsciously held and taught all the doctrines of John Huss. . . . We are all Hussites without knowing it."

If Luther was a Hussite without having been taught of Huss directly, he was a Wyclifite by the same token. Wyclif did not seize upon the Pauline justification by faith, and make it the all in all of Christianity, as Luther did. But in other respects the doctrines of the two men ran parallel, and also the circumstances of their lives. They both were nationalists or patriots, revolting against the abuses of a foreign papal church; and both of them as champions of their people won such popular support that they could defy papal bulls launched against them. Both took the same stand as to papal excommunications and interdicts; both assailed the pope as Anti-Christ and both held (though Luther only for a time) a conception of the Church as the Community of all the saints of God alive and dead. They were both active in affairs, working under a dominant impulse to destroy religious abuses; and both had the power of wrath as well as the power of speech. They both attacked papal indulgences and absolution, pilgrimages and the worship of relics; they both denounced the notion of the funded supererogatory merits of the saints making a treasury from which popes drew and distributed for value received. Both were hostile to the monks, and deemed their vows unsanctioned by Scripture; both thought that priests should marry. Both assaulted the doctrine of transubstantiation, Wyclif being the less conservative of the two; but on the other hand, Luther threw off the scholastic form in his writings more completely than Wyclif, who never rid himself of it when writing in Latin, but only when writing English. Both of them translated the Bible, or parts of it, into their native tongue, held Scripture to be the sole authority in religion, and denounced whatever went beyond it as unsanctioned and erroneous.[16] In expounding

---

15 Nov., 1530, De Wette, I. p. 356.

16 Wyclif's older contemporary Occam declares that popes and councils may err, and that Scripture only is infallible: ergo Christianus de necessitate salutis non tenetur ad credendum nec credere

Scripture, both sought the actual meaning, and made temperate use of allegorical interpretation. With both of them, their religious doctrines were of gradual growth: they were progressive in their "heresies." But unwarranted application of their teachings and peasant wars tended to make them conservative socially and politically in the end.[17]

Regarded from the standpoint of Church politics, the sixteenth century followed the period of the complete defeat of the so-called Conciliar Movement. The fifteenth had opened with the Church and papacy struggling out of the Great Schism, consequent upon the return of the popes from Avignon. Distinguished statesmen of the Church, the Frenchmen Gerson and D'Ailly, and after them the German Nicholas of Cusa, not to mention Gregor Heimburg, sought to subject the pope to the control of councils representative of the catholic nations. It was a time when councils deposed popes and attempted Church reforms. There was the Council of Pisa in 1409, and the great Council of Constance from 1414 to 1418. Finally came the Council of Basel, which dragged out its existence from 1431 to 1449. Its preposterous conduct, corruption, and palpable impotence abashed Nicholas of Cusa and other honest supporters of conciliar authority. Aided by international jealousy and the impossibility of concord among the churchmen of Spain, England, France and Germay, papal diplomacy triumphed. It had played off interest against interest, order against order, nation against nation. The threat of a general council might still be used to worry popes; but the politico-ecclesiastical incompetence of councils had been demonstrated. The Church was again a monarchy, gov-

---

quod nec in Biblia continetur nec ex solis contentis in Biblia potest consequentia necessaria et manifesta inferri. (Accordingly, a Christian is not obliged to subscribe to the Faith merely for the sake of his salvation, nor is he obliged to believe anything that is not in the Bible or that cannot be inferred from the Bible as an obvious and necessary conclusion.) See Seeberg, in *Protestantische Encyclopaedie,* article on Occam, p. 271.

[17] Wyclif will be spoken of more particularly in Vol. IV, Chap. 2.

erned by a papal Curia which was becoming completely Italian.

Never had the papacy been so glaringly and flauntingly secular as under an Alexander VI, a Julius II, or a Leo X. The effect of their reigns was to aggravate the mammon in the Church at large. The Church smacked always of this world; had at least its feet of clay. It existed on the fruits of the earth, and was at any epoch an exponent and expression of the time—in the fourth century, or in the twelfth, as well as in the fifteenth. In the early Middle Ages it became part of the feudal system so far as concerned its tenor and occupancy of land and the performance of its landed functions. Abbots and bishops held feudal rank, and usually were scions of noble or princely houses. This general condition of the Church did not pass with the Middle Ages. In Germany at the close of the fifteenth century, the higher ranks of the German clergy were filled with the sons of the nobility and the great benefices were held by princes.[18] Such a condition might prove fuel for peasant uprisings, but could not, like papal exactions, incite Germans to revolt against a foreign papal Church.

Before men revolt, they must distinguish and separate from themselves what they would revolt against. Everywhere the mediaeval clergy, with their practices and privileges, made part of the social structure of the country. If they enjoyed exemptions and exclusive rights, so did the nobles, so did the burghers of the towns. Law applying to all men was of slow and jealous growth. Special rights of a locality or an order, or even of individuals, existed everywhere, and when contested were contested by some other special right. Hence the peculiar privileges of the clergy did not seem to separate them from other classes of society, whose rights were likewise privileges. Some monarch or potentate, the king of France for instance, or the king of England, might have his quarrel with the pope, and yet the various orders of his realm might not feel themselves con-

18 Jansen, *Ges. des deutschen Volkes.*, Vol. I, p. 681 sqq. (seventeenth edition).

cerned as partisans. Such an affair was out of their sphere, went on above their heads.

In Germany, however, the conflict over the investiture of the clergy with their lands and offices was long and bitter. It seemed to center in a struggle between Emperors and popes, and tended to rouse national antipathy. The German clergy took one side or the other. But the struggle produced in the minds of the nobility and princes and their followers, a sense of antagonism to the papacy. That seemed a foreign foe, and not the less so when it intervened in German politics, in favor of one royal candidate as against another. From the thirteenth century, German antipathy to Rome is voiced by those great German voices, Walter von der Vogelweide and Freidank, whoever the latter was.[19] The current comes down the centuries, till it finds expression in the effective violence of an Ulrich von Hutten.

He was a knight; a thorny sprig of the German nobility. A hater of Rome, he became a truculent partisan of Luther on realizing that the latter had defied the pope. He cared not a whit for dogma or doctrine; but hated the papal power and the papal abominations imposed upon his fatherland. He fought with his pen, though he would have preferred fighting with the sword against the Italian usurper and extortioner.

If ever a book had struck hard against the temporal pretensions of the papacy, it was the book of Lorenzo Valla against the forged "Donation of Constantine." Erasmus's admiration for Valla, and the political situation, had brought this seventy-year-old writing to men's attention; and Hutten published it in 1517, with a preface of his own addressed to Leo X.[20] He never surpassed the insolent satire and mock adulation of this dedication. It had nothing to do with doctrine, and everything with false papal usurpations; and the same may be said of all Hutten's attacks upon the papacy. He speaks as a patriot, as a liberty-loving German, opposing alien tyranny. Thus for example in his *Vadiscus,* or his *Bulla vel Bullacida,* two violent invectives

---

19 Cf. *The Mediaeval Mind,* Vol. I, Chapter XXVII.
20 *Opera Hutteni,* ed. Boecking, Vol. I, pp. 155-161.

in the form of dialogues, belonging to the year 1520.[21]
Likewise in his fierce diatribes against Caracciollo and Aleander, the papal legates at the Diet of Worms, Hutten's
invective has nothing to do with doctrine: "You," he cries,
"all you Roman legates are robbers of our people, betray-
ers of Germany, destroyers of law and justice." [22] He in-
veighs as well against the higher Germany clergy: "Out
with ye, unclean swine, out from the holy place, ye truck-
sters; do ye not see that the air of freedom blows?" He
attacks even the Emperor Charles for bowing down before
the priests.

A somewhat more definite statement may be made of the
papal abuses which bore intolerably upon Germany at this
time. It will be recalled how enormous was the Church's
share in the landed property of Europe. The Church is reported to have owned a quarter of all the land; its revenues
vastly exceeded those of any king; it offered riches and
power to its bishops, abbots, and the rest of the higher
clergy, making a huge army, and all exempt from the jurisdiction of any court except the ecclesiastical. Limitations
upon the papal prerogative were uncertain and contested.
As watchful as it was elastic, that prerogative was prompt
to take advantage of weakness on the part of princes. In
1511, Julius II excommunicated the King and Queen of
Navarre, and offered their little Kingdom to whoever would
seize it. The popes had always claimed the right to grant
kingdoms and territories, to deprive rulers of their domains
and annul their subjects' allegiance. The exercise of papal
prerogatives forms a large part of mediaeval political history. The Church held a monopoly of salvation; and the
popes found that the keys of heaven and hell were mighty
levers to move the kingdoms of the earth. Diligently they
worked them. Through the century preceding the revolt of
Luther, the need felt by the popes to regain their power
after the Great Schism and the attacks of councils, combin-

[21] Both printed in Vol. IV. of Boecking's edition of Hutten:
Vadiscus dialogus qui et Trias Romana inscribitur, pp. 145-268;
Bulla &c., pp. 309-331.
[22] *Opera Hutteni,* Ed. Boecking, Vol. II, pp. 12-21.

ing with the tendencies of life and thought in Italy, went far toward making the papacy a sheer political institution. Its story for that century is one of effort to maintain and aggrandize its power, and prevent those ecclesiastical reforms which would have weakened its temporal resources and influence.

In the later Middle Ages, on through the fourteenth and the fifteenth centuries, into the sixteenth as well, the papacy put forth systematic claims to control the patronage of the universal Church. Popular protests and royal statutes were uncertain barriers to this sleepless encroachment upon the rights of local or national churches and of states. The papacy had abundant use for the enormously lucrative proceeds of this patronage. The expenses of the Holy See were great. In the time before us, the lavishness of Leo X led to that indiscreet and indecent sale of indulgences which drew out Luther's Theses. The papacy's extravagance made it a universal vendor of privileges and offices within its granting, of indulgences and marriage dispensations, of bishoprics and cardinalships.

Tithes and annates from the clergy were important sources of papal revenue. The annates, consisting of about half the annual value of a benefice, were exacted upon a change of the incumbent. They attached to every ecclesiastical holding, from a parish living of twenty-five florins value to the most opulent archbishoprics. It may be added that a good part of these revenues were absorbed in their collection. As fiscal agents of the papacy, the banking house of the Fuggers, at Augsburg, is said to have retained one half.

Germany was a convenient mine for the papacy. German kings and emperors had interposed so-called Pragmatic Sanctions and Concordats; but they could not, like the French or English kings, enforce the observance of them. And while the German princes could prevent abuses in their own dominions, they failed to unite in a protective antipapal policy. Hence the resistance from great personages, or from combinations of the clergy and laity could be effective only for the time and the occasion. The German grounds of complaint against the papacy, as set forth by public men or formulated by synods of the clergy or diets of the realm, have been termed *gravamina*. The so-called *Centum gravamina,* drawn up by the diet of Worms in 1521, are a *summa* of what had been stated from time to time through the preceding centuries. In substance they embrace: (1) Complaints over papal interference with elections to bishoprics and other church offices; over the bestowal of benefices on foreigners or on unfit Germans; and over the burdens placed upon the administration of the same. (2) Complaints over the grievous exactions for the papal revenue: annates and tithes and other matters. (3) Complaints over the papal judicial procedure, in that causes which should be decided in Germany were withdrawn to Rome, and there decided arbitrarily; also over exemptions granted by the Curia from the jurisdiction of German courts, both lay and spiritual, and over other abuses of ecclesiastical procedure.[23]

[23] See B. Gebhardt, *Die gravamina der deutschen Nation gegen den römischen Hof.* (Breslau 1895) passim, and especially pp. 103-113, and pp. 126 sqq.

Chapter 4

Martin Luther

I. FERMENT AND EXPLOSION

THE *Centum Gravamina,* spoken of at the close of the last chapter, summed up the German protests against the papal church. They reflected Luther's palpable atttitude toward the ecclesiastical, social, and political situation. Pointedly they corresponded with Luther's address *To the Christian nobility of the German nation,* which had appeared six months before.[1] It was one of Luther's most effective writings, and if so, one of the most immediately effective ever written by any man. Incisively, explicitly, constructively, set forth the ecclesiastical situation, and expressed the convictions, prejudices and antipathies of the nation. It brought sound doctrine and the truth of God to bear upon conditions grasped and presented by genius. A résumé of it will disclose those conditions and abuses which had already directed the yearnings and anxieties of Luther's religious nature into a torrent of revolt from Rome.

Having premised the necessity compelling so poor an individual to address their High Mightinesses, Luther opens with a warning not to rely on one's own power or wisdom, but on God. The Romanists have reared three walls around them, defenses against reform. They are

[1] Some of Luther's points touched other grievances and in a style unsuited to a state paper. See Gebhardt, *Gravamina &c.,* pp. 126-133.

these: First that the temporal power has no authority over the spiritual, but just the contrary; secondly, that no one except the pope may interpret the Scriptures; thirdly, that only the pope can call a council.

The first wall is overthrown by proof that the spiritual order is not composed of the pope alone, with his monks and bishops, but by all of us; for we are all a royal priesthood through baptism. Oil and tonsure make puppet idols; only baptism can make a Christian or a priest. Humanly the choice of priests lies with the Christian community. "For no one may take upon himself that which is common, without the mandate of the community. A priest is priest while he holds the office; he may be deposed, and then becomes peasant or burgher again. It follows that there is no distinction save that of office or function between laity and priests, between princes and bishops, between 'spiritual' and 'temporal' or worldly, as they are called. For all are members of the spiritual order, and really bishops, priests and popes, though they have not the same function; but neither has every priest and monk."

Now just as the "spiritual" are worthier than other Christians only because of their ministry, "so the temporal magistrates hold the sword and the rods that they may punish the wicked and protect the just. A shoemaker, a smith, a peasant, has the office of his handiwork; yet they are consecrated priests and bishops; and everyone should be useful and serviceable to the other, with his work or office, as all kinds of works are directed to serve the needs of one community, body and soul." It is for the temporal authorities to aid and punish priests, just as much as it is for shoemakers to make their shoes. Beyond their office, the alleged greater worth of the spiritual order is a human invention.

Think for yourselves, he bids his auditors, and recognize how preposterous is the notion that only the wicked pope may interpret Scripture, or call a council. The absurdity of the last idea grows as we consider the matters which councils properly may handle: to wit, the worldly pride of the pope with his three crowns, when the greatest king is content with one; the plundering of Germany and other countries, to find benefices for the cardinals, through which the land is wasted and the flock of Christ deprived of its pastors; the monstrous papal court which Germany helps to support by sending three hundred thousand gulden annually to Rome, and gets nothing in return—no wonder we are poor, but rather that we have not starved! "Here my complaint is not that God's command and Christian right is despised in Rome, for all is not so well in the rest of Christendom that we may make this high accusation. Neither do I complain that natural or temporal law and reason are made of no effect. The trouble lies deeper. I complain that Rome does not observe her own cunningly devised canon law, which in itself is tyranny, avarice, pride, rather than law."

The complaints thus far set forth were not novel. Other men had stated one or more of them before Luther, who now passes to more specific grievances. He begins with the Annates, and then points to one abusive exaction after another through which the pope and his cardinals plunder Germany. "How long will ye, ye noble princes and lords, leave your land open to such ravening wolves? . . . If Rome is not a brothel above all other brothels imaginable, I know not what a brothel is." There all things conceivable and inconceivable are done for gold. He refers briefly to other impositions—indulgences, permission to eat meat in Lent; and then proceeds to the remedies which the temporal power or a general council should prescribe. It will be enlightening to follow his points:

1. Let every prince, nobleman, and city forbid and abolish the annates.

2. Let them also see that no more benefices pass to the use of Rome.

3. Let an imperial edict prohibit bishops and other dignitaries from going to Rome for their installation; and forbid appeals to Rome in controversies: for now bishops and archbishops have no real power, but only the pope.

4. Prohibit the carrying of civil suits to Rome. What

touches the temporalities of the clergy may be decided before a consistory of German prelates; only let them not sell justice as it is sold at Rome.

5. Abolish the papal reservation of benefices upon the death of the incumbent; and if Rome send an unrighteous ban, let it be despised, as from a thief.

6. Abolish *casus reservati,* i.e. sins reserved for the pope to absolve from.

7. Let the Roman Curia abolish its useless offices and reduce its pomp.

8. Let the bishop no longer take those oaths that bind them to the Curia, and let the Kaiser resume the right of investiture.

9. Let the Kaiser cease to abase himself by kissing the pope's toe; and let the pope have only the authority over the Kaiser of a bishop who crowns and anoints him.

10. Let the pope surrender his claim to the Kingdom of Naples and Sicily and other principalities which do not belong to him.

11. Have done with kissing his feet; let him ride or walk and not be borne by men, and no longer receive the sacrament seated, from a kneeling cardinal offering it on a golden salver.

12. Let pilgrimages to Rome be abolished, not as evil in themselves, but because it is not well for pilgrims to see the wickedness of Rome. Pilgrimages after all are questionable; it is better for a man to attend to his duties at home.

13. Build no more cloisters for the Mendicants; let them stop their begging, preaching, and confessing.

14. The marriage of the clergy was not forbidden in apostolic times. "I advise that it again be made free and left to the discretion of each to marry or not." Especially the parish priests should be allowed to marry their housekeepers, with whom they live, and legitimatize their children.

15. Let the rules of confession for the wretched cloisters be changed, so that monks and nuns more freely may confess their secret sins.

16. Give up the masses and fixed prayers for the souls of the dead; which are done without love. "It is impossible that a work should be pleasing to God which is not done freely in love."

17. Abolish various ecclesiastical penalties, including the interdict.

18. Give up all saints' days, with their carousing, except Sundays.

19. Change the degrees within which marriage is forbidden; abolish fasts.

20. Tear down the forest chapels, where miracles occur for gold; give up pilgrim jaunts, and let God exalt the saints.

21. Forbid begging through Christendom; let each town care for its poor.

22. Abolish the new foundations for prayers and masses for departed souls.

23. Have done with papal dispensations and indulgences —a measure which Luther urges with telling invective against the pope, and a call on Christ to descend and destroy the devil's nest in Rome.

24. Come to an accord with the Bohemians, and recognize whatever truth and justice there may be in their convictions.

25. Reform the universities, where there is too much Aristotle and too little Christ. Throw out Aristotle's *Physics, Metaphysics,* and the rest of him, except his *Logic, Rhetoric,* and *Poetics,* which, in condensed form might be kept for elementary discipline. Maintain Latin, Greek and Hebrew, with mathematics and history. I leave it to the physicians to reform their faculty; but with regard to jurisprudence it were well to omit the Canon Law, especially the Decretals. There is enough in the Bible. As for our secular law, God help us, it is a jumble of territorial law and custom and imperial law. For the theologians, I say, let them give up the Sentences [of the Lombard] for the Bible, and reduce the number of treatises. Let the Bible be read in the schools.

26. The papacy professes to have taken the Empire

from the Greeks, and to have handed it over to the Germans. But the pope has our goods and honor, our bodies, lives and souls! Nevertheless, though the papacy took the Empire dishonestly, we have honestly received it: let us rule and manage it in freedom, not as slaves of the pope. Let the German Emperor be emperor indeed, in right and freedom.

27. For ourselves, we are luxurious and extravagant. We should be as well off with less trade and commerce. It were better to have more agriculture. And alas for our excesses in eating and drinking, for which we Germans have such ill repute abroad. Finally, alas for the houses of ill-fame among us! and alas also for their complement, the mistaken vows of chastity, on the part of monks and nuns and priests, which so few can keep! I have spoken boldly; perhaps too sharply. But it is better to anger the world than God!

In the power of its wrathful reason, the address to the German nobility is Luther truly, and yet Luther speaking as a German. It shows him as an element in a situation, and serves to introduce us to him through his participation in the convictions and detestations of his people. It is far from an expression of his innermost self, or of the needs, anxieties, and impulses which first drove him into a convent and then drove him out from the bounden way of living which brought no rest to his soul. His nature was religious fundamentally; its anxieties and impulses hung on his soul's relationship to God. To all this he gave convincing utterance in his tract upon *The Freedom of a Christian,* the pronunciamento of his very self. But before examining that writing, it were well to remember the lines of antecedents which drew together into this burning nature, and then observe the youthful fermentation preceding the explosion.

The inner verity (or falsity!) and outward facts of Luther's life—themes of whole libraries! Of outward facts it will be recalled that he was born at Eisleben in 1483 of well-to-do peasant stock. While he was a baby, his parents moved to the neighboring town of Mansfield, where mining was the chief industry. His father became a miner, a work for which the boy Martin showed himself unfit; the mines impressed him as murky places where devils bewitch and fool men with pockets of false ore, which were not so easy in the light of day. From his childhood to his dying day Luther believed in devils present and perceptible, perplexing men and hindering them, filling them with wicked doubts and devilish fears. One remembers his circumstantial story of devils throwing hazel nuts at him in bed in his chamber at the Wartburg.

In due course he was sent away from home to schools (of which he has little good to say) at Magdeburg, and then at Eisenach, where his pleasing boy's voice, singing in the street for his supper, won him the affection of Frau Cotta, wife of a prosperous merchant. When seventeen he entered the flourishing university of Erfurt. There he pursued philosophy of the scholastic type, adhering to the popular and progressive nominalism of Occam. A band of youthful humanists were gathering there at Erfurt. But Luther was never tempted toward classicism of style, though his earliest letters are not free from current humanistic phrases. He read the usual Latin authors, and became as ready with that tongue as he was with his mother German. It is not recorded that he was addicted to reading the Bible, or noticeably affected by religion. At the end of a year he received his Bachelor's degree, and three years later was made a magister with some éclat. He entered now upon the study of law, for which his father intended him.

But something happened to him, or perhaps had already happened, or been prepared, within him. In July, 1505, near Erfurt, he was caught in a heavy thunderstorm, and cried out: "Help, good St. Anna, I will become a monk." Something within him, beyond physical terror, must have responded to the thunder. It was the moment, or occasion, of his conversion. He announced his purpose, bade formal farewell to his friends, and entered the Augustinian convent there at Erfurt. The town had seven other monasteries, and he chose well; for the Augustinian convent was pious and orderly, given to preaching and clean living; and had the admirable Staupitz for its head. Luther found there nothing to make him waver. He had fifteen months to consider his decision before taking the final vows. In the year following that event he was ordained priest (1507).

Luther's convent life passed in study and strenuous observance. He devoted himself to scholastic theology and philosophy, still following Occam, in whose system lay much disintegrating criticism of the whole scholastic structure. He also studied the works of Peter D'Ailly, a broadminded churchman, who favored the authority of Councils, and those of Gabriel Biel, an influential German scholastic who had recently died. He began a close reading of the Bible, which was not as yet to bring him certitude or peace. What was taking place in his mind? It was tortured with anxieties and fears beyond the understanding of his fellows. But one should not think of him as on the verge of religious melancholia; for a mental condition which might to-day denote weak reason and a neurotic temperament, had no such significance in the early sixteenth century, when the most intelligent were still justified by their intellectual environment in entertaining a lively fear of hell. In Luther's personality a powerfully reasoning faculty and an immense rational perception were united with emotional energy and that religious or self-depreciating temperament which contemplates human destinies as dependent on a mightiest being, and deems its salvation to lie in obedient union with that Being. Thus Luther's mind was held in dilemmas of its general education and doctrinal instruction, and its furthest spiritual intuitions. It was tormented by its sinfulness and inability to attain a righteousness that should unite him with the Being in whom was its salvation. The young Luther was endeavoring punctiliously to fulfil the righteousness of a monk; but his life, exemplary to others' eyes, seemed to him infected with shortcomings and frustration. Deep spasms of unhappiness came over him. One may also remember that he was twenty-five years old, and of a temper that might be prone to the ardors of the flesh.

In 1508 the watchful Staupitz procured Luther's call to Wittenberg, to teach logic and ethics of the Aristotelian brand in the Saxon Elector's new university. But before many months elapsed he returned to the Erfurt convent in order to teach or study theology. In 1511 Staupitz sent him with a brother monk on an errand to Rome. There his heart filled with reverence for the Eternal City with its myriad tombs and relics of the martyred saints; but he was shocked, as any earnest inexperienced German would have been, by the worldliness and immorality of the clergy. After his return in 1512 he settled permanently in the Augustinian convent at Wittenberg, to teach theology and philosophy at the university, which now made him a doctor of theology. He called himself Professor of Holy Scripture. Preaching was soon added to his duties; he had the gift for this, though at first he spoke with trepidation. In 1515 he was made district vicar of his Order, an office which put eleven monasteries under his care. His life had ceased to be that of a recluse monk; he had become a man of varied duties among men, with a huge correspondence, and the beginnings of a prodigious literary activity. No greater preacher had appeared in Germany; and never was there so great a pamphleteer as Luther became. His occupations freed him from the danger of morbidity, and with his studies and lecturing, promoted the growth of all his faculties.

Luther's first lecture course was upon the Psalms. The next year he took up Paul's Epistle to the Romans, and in expounding it, learned much for himself, as he says, "saw the light." He continued with a course on Galatians. According to the traditional interpretation concurred in by Erasmus, Paul's "works of the law" referred to Jewish ceremonies. Luther maintained that Paul meant the whole moral law included in the Decalogue.[2] It mattered little if

2 Letter to Spalatin of Oct. 19, 1516—De Wette's Edition, I, p. 39. My references to Luther's letters are to this edition.

man could fulfil the minutiae of a ceremonial abrogated by Christ; but it was quite a different affair to become convinced that no man could fulfil the unabrogated moral law of God. This conviction appears to have driven Luther to take refuge with Paul in salvation through faith.

As Luther had little knowledge of Greek or Hebrew, he was obliged to use the Vulgate. He sought guidance in the works of the Church Fathers, especially Augustine; and also studied the commentary of Nicholas of Lyra, and the very recent work of Lefvre of Etaples.[3] Besides which, he read Tauler and the *Theologia Deutsch*. In 1516 appeared Erasmus' edition of the Greek New Testament, and Luther set himself to master that tongue. His mind always pressed for the best scholarship on the subjects holding his interest; before this, he had spoken out boldly for Reuchlin, against the bigots of Cologne. He cared little for Aquinas and his school; and began to abjure their pagan master, Aristotle. His influence was already felt by his friends at Wittenberg, among whom was Carlstadt, whose later radical views were to prove such a thorn in Luther's side. By May, 1517, he speaks of "our theology" as progressing, while Aristotle is declining to defeat.

Naturally Luther's keen mind perceived the follies of sundry religious practices, while his increasing knowledge of men and affairs acquainted him with the corruption in the priesthood and the monastic orders. He began to think pilgrimages foolish, and to say so in his sermons. While not as yet condemning in principle the worship of the saints, he protested vigorously, as Erasmus did, against the preposterous prayers which they were asked to grant; and he showed the silliness of some of their legends. He was painfully impressed with the dearth of true Gospel preaching in the Church.

Through the crying corruption of an institution, one may be led to denounce the institution itself on principle. It was thus with Luther in regard to indulgences. As early as July,

[3] Cf. above p. 31 and Vol. III, Chap. 8.

1516, he spoke with some uncertainty against abuses of the practice. And in later sermons through that year and the first half of the next, he continued his attack upon their pernicious effects, while still recognizing their legitimate basis in the merits of Christ and the saints. Indulgences indeed were very old, and, within limits, justified by good church doctrine. It had long been held that sins committed after baptism could be blotted out only through the sacrament of penance. Repentance, confession to a priest, and acts in atonement were required. The priest pronounced absolution from eternal punishment, yet the satisfaction of penitential acts must be rendered, to relieve the sinner from punishment in purgatory. Various forms of penance were allowed: one could go on a crusade, or undertake less dangerous pilgrimages; then there were fasts and scourgings, and at last the payment of money. The souls of the dead might be released from purgatory by money payments. In the popular mind, and often by the connivance of the clergy, such payments freed the sinner from all the evil consequences of his sins.

This system appeals to many instincts, and, considering the level of intelligence through the Middle Ages, one realizes that the Church could not have maintained moral discipline by any more spiritual means. The old *wergeld* was in the blood; men understood penance and absolution upon atonement, payment—the painful costly act, or the money handed to the priest. Righteousness through faith alone would have been intangible.

By the sixteenth century, men had become more intelligent, and the abuses of the penitential system appeared grosser, and, in fact, had become more pronounced and demoralizing. In the famous instance before us, Pope Leo X, needing money to complete St. Peter's, proclaimed a "plenary indulgence" offering sweeping benefits to purchasers; and the impecunious Hohenzollern Albrecht, Archbishop of Mainz, bargained with the pope to manage the sale of indulgences in Germany on shares. Tetzel, a Dominican, was his agent. Now be it marked that the campaign of Tetzel, whose approach to Wittenberg roused Luther to post those famous Theses, had already led Duke George of Saxony, stanchest of Catholics, to forbid the sale within his territory. The great Elector too, Luther's Elector Frederic, had forbidden Tetzel to enter his part of Saxony. But without crossing the Saxon border, Tetzel had come near enough to draw many good Wittenbergers to his sale.

Luther devoted some months of study and reflection to the whole matter of penance and indulgences; and on the last day of October, 1517, he posted on the door of the Castle church the notice of a disputation together with the ninety-five propositions, or theses, which he proposed to maintain.

These began with a statement that when Christ commanded repentance he meant that the entire life of the believer should be a state of penitence. Passing on from this broad premise, the Theses, point by point, or rather blow on blow, demonstrated the futility of the sale and purchase of indulgences, and attacked the heart of the papal, or Catholic, penitential system. For example: the pope can remit only those punishments which he has prescribed in accord with sound doctrine: when the coin clinks in the box, though avarice may gain, forgiveness still depends on God; whoever thinks that the Indulgence makes his salvation sure, is damned eternally with those who taught him so; every Christian who lives in true repentance has complete remission of his sins, without any letter of indulgence; true penitence loves punishment, the indulgence marks its rejection; he does better who gives his money to the poor; the indulgences issuing from the so-called treasury of the Church makes the last first; Christ's gospel is the true treasure of the church, and makes the first last.

The doctrinal details of this controversy are no longer of interest. But the conflict was important for the world, being the obvious occasion of Luther's rupture with the papal church; for himself it was important as a stage in the attainment of his spiritual freedom; a fact of which he seems to have been conscious, since he now took to signing himself in letters to his friends, Martin Eleutherius, or Martin the Free. There is no need to speak of the storm of enthusiasm as well as condemnation, which the Theses roused, loosed, one might say. Germany was stirred; so were the indulgence sellers and papal advocates, and in time the papacy itself. Thousands of books have told the story, not always quite in the same words! The course of the dispute educed the steadfast intrepidity of Luther's nature, and served to show him where he stood and perforce must stand. Thus his defense before the papal legate Cajetan at Augsburg, his argument with the more deft and understanding Miltitz, the formal disputation with Doctor Eck at Leipzig, the lowering and certain papal excommunication, and at last its fall, all helped to evoke the man and propel him onward to the final freeing of his spirit. Friends and adherents anxiously upheld his hands, and the protection of his prince prevented his bodily snuffing out by papal legates.

II. Luther's Freeing of His Spirit

A man whom the papal catholic church sought to annihilate, and who on his side was preparing to cast loose from it, would feel the need to justify and strengthen his steps. Luther felt as well the deeper need to make firm his convictions touching his new assurance of salvation, which was grounded, and had its height and depth, in faith, and had freed his soul not only from the salvation which the papal church claimed to monopolize, hierarchically and sacerdotally as it were, but also from the bondage of the works which the Church held needful for every one that should be saved. Thus, bold within his soul and for the edification of the world, Luther had to establish a justification of his severance from the papal church, and the grounds of his saving faith.

Since the papal ban was about to fall on him, his first task was to demonstrate its nullity. Shortly after posting his

Theses he had spoken on this, but by no means finally. Afterwards, returning to the subject (1519), he wrote a sermon on the Holy Sacrament of the Communion, as preparatory to the examination of the obviously connected *excommunicatio* which he considered in his weighty "Sermon on the Ban," written in 1519, and published early in the next year. He argues thus: As the Sacrament is both sign and significance, so is the Communion twofold. Priest or pope cannot sever the believer from the spiritual communion which rests in faith, though he may be excluded from outer participation in the Sacrament. This was the lesser excommunication. When extended to the prohibition of all intercourse as well as Christian burial, it became the greater excommunication. Later it carried with it fire and sword, thus going beyond Scripture, which leaves the sword to secular authorities. An excommunicated person may be forbidden the Sacrament and even deprived of burial, and yet be safe and blessed in the Communion of Christ. Conversely, many who are admitted to the Sacrament may be in a state of spiritual separation. No excommunication has the effect of delivering the soul into hell, though, when deserved, it may be a sign that the faithless soul has given itself over to the devil through its sins. The object of the excommunication is to bring the damned soul back. Christians should honor and love it as the warning punishment of motherly love. So the sermon showed that even a rightful excommunication should not be regarded as an object of terror; while an unjust ban was a spiritual nullity. After Luther's excommunication, the latter point received adequate treatment in his polemic, *Against the Bull of the Antichrist.*

With his mind settled as to the spiritual impotence of papal bulls, the ills which might happen to his body could safely be left with God and the secular powers. He was a fearless man. But now while his opponent Dr. Eck was publishing the Bull in Saxony, Luther launched a mighty blow at the papal edifice, from which he had just emerged, or been ejected. At the close of his *Address to the German*

Nobility, he had announced another little song about Rome and about his enemies who would accept no peace from him, and loud would he sing it. If the *Address* had breached those three walls with which Rome had bulwarked her corruption, he would now shatter her inner defenses and the armory where she forged her weapons and the chains in which she held the Church. In fine, it was the papal sacramental system that he sought to destroy by this *Prelude upon the Babylonian Captivity of the Church.* As his argument dealt largely with dogma, he chose to write the piece in Latin.

"I learn more every day, as I must, since so many clever masters push me on,"—says Luther, mockingly. "And now would that what I have written on indulgences might be burnt, so that I might simply declare: indulgences are a vain invention of the Roman Flatterer. Eck and his like have taught me such things of the pope's high mightiness, that I could also throw away whatever I have written on that matter; for now I see that the papacy is Babylon, the dominion of the mighty hunter, the sheer dumping ground of the bishop of Rome."

The sacraments are not seven, but three, Baptism, Penance, and the Eucharist; and indeed Penance should be excluded if a sacrament is a promise coupled with a sign. The Eucharist is held captive first through the pope's godless withholding of the cup from the laity, whose conscience craves it; secondly through the doctrine of transubstantiation; thirdly, by the teaching that the mass is a sacrifice and a good work. But neither the pope nor even a general council can make new articles of belief. In the celebration of the mass, only faith is needed, faith in Christ promising forgiveness of sins to those who believe that his body and blood were given for them.

Through baptism, he who believes and is baptized will be saved: the belief is everything; the act is but the outer sign, carrying no saving virtue. But the freedom of our baptism is led captive by the pope through set prayers and fasts and gifts. And as for further vows, would that all

those of monks and nuns and pilgrimages could be swept
away; for they impugn the freedom of baptism, wherein
indeed we undertook more than we ever shall fulfil! All
rash vows, and vows of the young should be held void. The
pope alone can dispense vows! Absurd! Everyone may,
for his neighbor or himself. But neither the pope nor another can dispense from the holy vows of marriage. Divorce
is such an abomination that bigamy were better. Nor has
the pope authority to invent artificial impediments, for the
breach of which, unless he dispense them, the marriage
may be dissolved. Yet marriage is not a sacrament, since
it carries no promise and exacts no faith. Neither is confirmation, ordination, or extreme unction. As for penance
(whether it be a sacrament or not), its virtue which lies in
the divine promise and our faith, has been made null by
prescribed works of repentance, confession and atonement.
Whereupon Luther returns to his attack upon indulgences.

The "Babylonian Captivity of the Church" was for
Luther himself, and for all the world, a sufficiently emphatic declaration of the Christian's independence of the
papacy and its sacramental monopoly. But it did not contain the demonstration of that fuller freedom of the human
spirit which lies in the certitude of man's salvation in his
direct relationship with God through Christ. A broad
foundation for this freedom was laid in Luther's sermon
On good works, written in the early part of 1520. Those
only are good works which are commanded by God; only
those acts which He has forbidden are sins. The first and
noblest of good works is faith, without which prayers,
fasts, pious foundations and all outer acts, are vain. With
faith every daily act of life and business is good; and everyone knows when he does right by the inner confidence that
his act is pleasing to God. Any work done without faith
might be done by Turk or heathen, Jew or sinner. Faith is
not to be classed with other works, since it alone makes all
other works good, and brings with it love, peace, joy, hope.
In faith, distinctions between works fall away, and all
works are equally good, since they are good and pleasing to

God not in themselves but through faith in His word. Doubt leads the Christian to distinguish between works and question which is better. Only faith comforts us in our works, sorrows, and disappointments and dispels the thought that God has forsaken us, even when we stand in prospect of death and fear of hell.

Works without faith justify no one in the sight of God. Our works are praiseworthy only through our faith that they are pleasing to Him. Had every one faith, no laws would be needed. All things and works are free to a Christian through his faith; but because others do not yet believe, he works with them, and suffers them, freely, knowing that this pleases God. Thus the freedom of faith is no freedom to do evil, harmful acts. And Luther proceeds to set forth in detail that excellence of living which comes with faith in Christ and accords with the commands of God.

Such is the foundation of the freedom which Luther sought for himself and for every man. But in the tract upon the "Freedom of the Christian Man" written also in 1520, Luther completes the structure of this freedom, and indicates the way his mind had reached it; as Paul set forth in the Epistle to the Galatians the way of freedom which he had found, and now declared to them.

Miltitz, a gentleman of the world as well as a papal agent, seeing the dangers involved in the Lutheran revolt, sought a means of truce. He tried to persuade Luther into some sort of submission to the pope, perhaps unaware as yet of the vast truculence of Luther's nature. In the autumn of 1520 when Luther in fact was under excommunication, Miltitz asked him to write a letter to the pope and dedicate a conciliatory work to him. The request bore other fruit! Luther wrote a letter and prefixed it to *The Freedom of the Christian Man,* which was nearly through the press, antedating both the letter and the treatise, that they might not seem to have been written under the pressure of the ban. Indeed they scarcely would have given that impression. The letter was written in Latin and German, while the treatise was written in German, but was shortly followed by a Latin translation bearing the title *Tractatus de libertate Christiana.*[4]

Luther begins his letter with an elaborate protestation that he has never said a word against His Holiness, and has always spoken of him with the respect felt by all. Indeed he had called Leo a Daniel in Babylon! He had, to be sure, attacked certain impious doctrines, and those who maintained them. Yet he will be found pliable and yielding, except as to the word of God, by which he must stand. True it is, continues Luther, that I have attacked your Chair, which is called the Curia; but no one knows better than yourself that its state is worse than Sodom or Gomorrah or Babylon! And I am grieved that in your name and that of the Roman Church, they have betrayed and robbed the poor throughout the world. I will stand against that! None is better aware than you, that for years nothing but corruption of body, soul, and estate has come out of Rome: all the people see that the once holy Roman church has become a den of cutthroats and a house of shame, of death and damnation! And you, Holy Father, sit as a sheep among wolves!

The writer goes on, pouring the vials of his wrath upon the papacy, with revilings not unlike those in the letter which Hutten prefixed to Valla's book on the forged "Donation of Constantine." "It is for you and your cardinals to cure this woe. But the disease laughs at the physic. . . . This is why I am sad, you pious Leo, to see you pope, for you are worthy of being pope in better times. The Roman chair is not fit for such as you: the evil spirit ought to be pope. . . . Would to God, you would resign this honor, as your spiteful enemies call it. . . . O thou most unhappy Leo, seated on the most perilous of chairs! . . ."

"See, my lord Father, this is why I have struck at this

---

4 The German Title "Von der Freiheit eines Christenmenschen" is usually rendered into English as "the freedom of a Christian man," perhaps the best rendering, if one will bear in mind that *Mensch* means human being. Both versions of the letter are given in De Wette, Vol. I, pp. 497 sqq.

pestilential chair so violently. I had hoped to have earned your thanks. I thought it would be a blessing to you and many others to rouse intelligent and learned men against the ruinous disorder of your court. They who attack such a Curia do the work which you should do; they honor Christ who put that court to shame." In fine, those are good Christians who are bad Romans!—And for me, when I had thought to keep silence, and had said 'Adieu! sweet Rome, stink on'; then the devil set on his servant Eck to drag me to a disputation! But that I should recant, and submit to be ruled in the interpretation of God's word, which is freedom,—never! As for thee, trust not those who would exalt thee as its sole interpreter; but honor those who would bring thee down. I, who cannot flatter, am forced to come to thy aid, and not with empty hands, but with a little book.—and Luther presents him *The Freedom of a Christian Man*.

The letter to Leo was written as a letter to Leo; but the little book which Luther as an afterthought presented him, was written to set forth for himself and those who might hold with him, the moving convictions of his spiritual freedom. The soul of Paul lives in this German sixteenth century book, which opens with a lofty Pauline paradox: "A Christian is a free lord over all things, and subject to no man. A Christian is a bounden servant to all things, and subject to everyone."

The solid reasoning of Luther's argument will best be brought out by following it point by point, on to its veritable attainment.

A Christian is both spirit and body. After the first he is a spiritual, new, and inner man; according to flesh and blood, he is a corporeal, old, outer man. Hence the scripture paradox, that he is both bond and free.

In so far as he is a spiritual inner man, no outer thing can make him pious and free. For piety and freedom, or their opposites, are not of the outer man. That the body is free and satisfied, or the reverse, neither helps nor hurts the soul.

The soul is not helped when the body puts on holy garb,

frequents churches, prays, fasts, or does any good work; for an evil man can do all this. Nor is the soul injured when the body abstains from all this.

The soul needs only the holy Gospel, the word of God preached by Christ; she has food and joy and light and truth, wisdom and freedom in that.

In that word thou shalt hear thy God telling thee that thy life and works are nothing in God's sight, but must eternally perish (ewiglich verderben). Believing in thy guiltiness, thou must despair of thyself, and with firm faith give thyself to God's dear Son and trust in him. Then thy sins will be forgiven thee through faith, thy destruction (verderben) vanquished, and thou wilt be righteous, at peace, with all commands fulfilled, and free from all things, as St. Paul says (Rom. 1, 17; 10, 4).

Therefore the true work and practice for Christians lies in building up Christ and the word within them, and in constantly strengthening their faith.

Faith alone, without works, makes righteous. Scripture consists in commands and promises. The former belong to the Old Testament, and bring no strength to fulfil them, which we cannot do.

Then the man despairs. But the divine promise assures him; if thou wilt fulfil all, and be free from sin and from desire of evil, believe on Christ in whom I promise thee grace and righteousness, peace and freedom. Believing, thou hast; unbelieving, thou hast not. God alone commands; and God alone fulfils. The promises are God's words in the New Testament.

"These and all words of God are holy, true, righteous, peaceful, free, and full of all good things; therefore, whosoever cleaves to them in right faith, his soul is so entirely united with them, that all the virtues of the word become the soul's, and through faith the soul is by God's word holy, righteous, peaceful, free and full of all good things, a true child of God. . . . No good work cleaves to God's word like faith, nor can be in the soul, where only the word and faith can reign. What the word is, that the soul becomes through the word, as iron becomes glowing red as the fire, through union with it. Hence one sees faith is sufficient for the Christian; he needs no work in order to be righteous. If then he needs no work, he is assuredly loosed from all commands and laws." [5]

To believe in God is to honor Him: to disbelieve is to dishonor Him. When God sees the soul thus honoring Him, He honors the soul, and holds it righteous.

Faith joins the soul to Christ, as bride to bridegroom. They become one. All the good things of Christ becomes the soul's, and the sins and negligences of the soul become Christ's. All sins are swallowed up in Christ's invincible righteousness.

Faith fulfils all commands, and makes righteous; for it fulfils the First Commandment, to honor God, and that fulfils them all. "But works are dead things, which cannot honor and praise God, though they may be done in His honor. Here we seek not that which is done like the works, but the doer and workman who honors God and does the works. That is none other than the heart's faith, which is the head and entire being of piety. (Frömmigkeit.) Therefore it is a dangerous dark saying, when one exhorts to fulfil the commands of God with works, since the fulfilment must take place through faith before all works; and the works follow the fulfilment, as we shall hear."

In the Old Testament, God reserved the first born male of man and beast, and gave him lordship and priesthood. This was a symbol of Christ, to whom is given the spiritual priesthood and kingship; which he shares with all who believe on him. Hence spiritually we are lords over all things, not as bodily possessing them, but as spiritually made free regarding them.

Through faith all believers are priests and intercessors, and lords of all, through God's power, who does their will; and we need nothing, and have abundance—spiritu-

---

[5] I use quotation marks here, because I have translated this passage in full. Elsewhere I have usually condensed the substance of the tract.

ally. We lose it by thinking to achieve it by good works, and not through faith.

In Christendom, priests are distinguished from laity merely as ministers of the word and servers, with no further privilege over other Christians.

It is not enough for the preacher to tell the story of Christ; he must make plain all that Christ is to us; through whom we are kings and priests, with lordship over all things, and freed from the works of the Law, our sins taken by Christ, and his righteousness ours through faith.

But men are not all spirit; not altogether the inner man. We are also bodies. Thus the Christian is the servant of all, and bound to the service of all. Let us see.

Though we are "inner" men, justified through faith, yet we continue in this bodily life, associating with other men. Here works begin; and the body must be practised in good works, that it may conform to faith and the inner man, and not cause him to stumble. The inner man is one with God, and joyful in the doing of Christ's will in love freely; but he finds a contrary will in his own flesh, willing the lusts of the world, which faith cannot endure, as Paul saith.

Works must not be done in the thought that they make the man righteous before God; but voluntarily, and freely, to please God; as Adam did what pleased God, while still righteous in Eden.

Thus it is truly said, just works do not make a just man; but a just man does just works. Nor do evil works make an evil man; but an evil man does evil works.

Conversely, good works will not save one who is without faith; nor will evil works bring him to perdition, but his unbelief. So it is vain and damnable to rely on works, or preach them uncoupled with faith.

As toward men, our works must be done in love. My God has given to me, utterly worthless and damned, righteousness and salvation through Christ, *so that henceforth I need only to believe that this is so*. I will act toward my neighbor likewise. So the Virgin, after Christ's birth, went to the Temple for her purification; not that she was impure, but did it freely out of love, so as to show no contempt for other women. And so Paul circumcised Timothy. On like grounds, we should be subject to the authorities.

Thus no work is good, unless its end is to serve another. Few cloisters, churches, masses, have been founded or endowed from love, but rather, vainly, to cure the founder's sins. Freely must the good things of God flow from one to another of us.

"From all this, the conclusion follows that a Christian does not live unto himself, but in Christ and his neighbor: in Christ through faith, in his neighbor through love. Through faith he ascends above himself in God, and through love passes out from God again beneath himself, yet abides always in God and godlike love. . . . Behold, that is the true, spiritual Christian freedom which frees the heart from all sins, laws and commands, which surpasses all other freedom as the heaven the earth. This may God give us truly to understand and keep. Amen."

So love and service of one's neighbor are made the criterion and sanctification of all the Christian's acts. His conduct shall not be hampered and harassed by anxieties regarding his sinlessness, holiness, aloofness from the dross of life. He does not need the safeguard of monastic vows: let him marry and beget children, or bear them if the Christian be a woman. Let the two take part in the business of life, plant and hoe and cook unpestered with vows and fasts and pilgrimages, so long as their lives are useful and do not cause their neighbor to stumble. Righteousness needs no other guaranty than faith, and the motive of useful service springing from it.

The incidents of Luther's life, which have been mentioned and the writings that have been analyzed, indicate the progress of his convictions until the time of his revolt and excommunication. To recapitulate: we know little of the experiences of his mind during his years at school and at the Erfurt university. But we know that from the time of his apparently sudden conversion he felt acute anxious-

ness over his sinfulness and consequent perdition. Life in
the Augustinian convent consisted in conformity to a
moral and religious code, in the observance of monastic
rules, and the performance of incidental or occasional
duties. Luther found that he could not clear his conscience
and assure himself of salvation by the strictest fulfilment
of these requirements, any more than Paul could satisfy
his mind and justify himself by his efforts to do the work
of the Law. Spiritual certitude was an imperative need
with both. Paul, perhaps in that spiritually fruitful sojourn
in Arabia (Gal. 1, 17) cast off the saving agency of works
and ensconced himself in the principle of faith in Christ
Jesus. Luther in the early years of his professorship at
Wittenberg (1512-16) following the example and the
doctrine of Paul, accepted faith in Christ as the sole means
and principle of salvation. It was a saving grace flowing
directly from the Saviour to the sinner, without the intervention of any pope or priest, who to Luther's mind were
prescribers of the outer act, the good work, the work of
the Law, and were guarantors of its efficacy, which Luther
had disproved in himself. So in accepting faith as the sole
principle of salvation, he virtually freed himself both from
the need of the visible church and from its authority.

He had accomplished this for himself, and had im-
parted some of the freedom of his faith to his associates
and pupils, by the year 1516 or 1517. Then Tetzel came
with his indulgences. Luther was aroused to a protest
pregnant with defiance and revolt, by the abominable
nature of this bartered and sold salvation, and by the
realization that it directly countered salvation through faith,
which he had reached by grace and not through money.
Had there been no abuse, Luther would not have been
stung to an open attack first upon the abuse and then upon
the doctrine; but might have kept on quietly teaching
salvation through faith. The sale of indulgences, which was
his call to action, made clear to him his strength and independence. The posting of his Theses, and their astound-

ing reception, impressed him with his rôle and duty to act for his Germans too.

The angry controversy which followed served to clear his thoughts, expand his arguments, and demonstrate the need to abandon other practices and tenets of the papal church. Moreover, the war against indulgences pushed on this very willing man to champion the cause of his Germans against Rome; and as the fray progressed he carried them along with him, from point to point, to ever clearer opposition to the papal church. He frees them, as he frees himself, from subjection to the papal hierarchy, and from the system of salvation which depends on priestly mediation and consists so largely in the performance of acts prescribed by priestly authority. Thus from denunciation of the abuse he advances to emphatic opposition to the institution from which the abuse had emanated, and emancipates his people, all stirred with German wrath against Rome, from Papal authority, and leads them on into that freedom of the Christian which is through faith alone. As a result, the imperial unity of the Roman Catholic church is broken, and the way laid open to other kinds of intellectual freedom with which Luther might have had scant sympathy.

III. THE FURTHER EXPRESSION OF THE MAN

The dynamic quality of religion is exhaustless. Man's conception of relationship to the divine Might, on Which or Whom his life and eternal destinies depend, constantly renews and manifests itself in all his faculties; it moulds his purposes and inspires his action. It seems to be the energy of God in man. It was so in Paul, so in Augustine, in Anselm, Bernard, Francis. It was so in Luther. There was a rebirth of Christianity in all these men. Luther had no more doubt than Paul that a personal revelation of God had come to him, and a divine call; and that Christ was actually reborn in him. The last thought might have come to him from the *Theologia Deutsch* as well as from his greatest teacher, Paul, who in another than a mystic sense was likewise reborn in Luther. Once more the power of the Gospel was shown, energizing and directing the nature and faculties of Luther, and spending its surplus force in the picturesque doings of Anabaptists for example, and the Peasants' War, where it worked along with other causes.

Luther was guided more directly by Paul than by the Sermon on the Mount. Yet he deemed himself to be following all the Scriptures, assuredly the Ten Commandments, assuredly the passion of the Psalmist, assuredly the teachings of his Lord in the four Gospels. Besides his almost superhuman grasp of Paul, he continued the strain of Gospel piety which appears in mediaeval saints. He says substantially in his *Table Talk:* Let no one stumble over the simple tales in Scripture; they are the very words and works and judgments of God. This is the book that makes fools of little wiselings. Thou shalt find in it the angels who guided the shepherds and the swaddling clothes and cradle in which Jesus lay: mean and wretched, but how precious the treasure, Christ, which lies in them. These phrases might be Bernard's as well as Luther's, and so might be many passages in Luther's letters. Do we not almost hear Bernard in the following to Spalatin, written in 1519: Quicumque velit salubriter de Deo cogitare aut speculari, prorsus omnia postponat praeter humanitatem Christi. Hanc autem vel agentem vel patientem sibi praefigat, donec dulcescat ejus benignitas.[6] Again: thou shalt find peace only in Him, through faithful despairing of thyself and thy work—per fiducialem desperationem tui et operum tuorum.[7] One notes that this sweet piety, whether of Francis, Bernard, or Luther, is filled with faith.

[6] (Whoever wishes to meditate and reflect on God in a wholesome manner, let him turn his back on all things, save the humanity of Christ. Let him have this ever before himself, both in work and in suffering, until the full sweetness of Christ comes to him.) De Wette's Edition, Vol. I, p. 226.

[7] To Spenlein, ib. p. 17; Cf. to Scheurl, ib. p. 49. Letters of 1516 and 1517.

In his study of the Bible, Luther sought the veritable meaning of the text. The downrightness of his nature would have led him to this, even if he had not been influenced by the comments of Nicholas de Lyra and Johann Wessel.[8] More and more he was repelled by the strained and twisted applications which were made to support those teachings, practices, or institutions of the papal church which he found himself revolting from. Yet no more than Erasmus did he give over the allegorical interpretation of the Old Testament, or even of the New. But he looked in the New Testament for confirmation of allegorical interpretations of words and statements in the Old.[9] He makes fewer references to allegorical meanings in his later writings, referring to himself as early as December, 1522, as "being already less curious regarding allegories."[10] To be sure, like any student of the Scriptures, in any age, with doctrines to uphold, Luther could bend the meaning to his own support.

Inevitably Luther judged the different books of the Bible by their bearing on the Gospel of faith in Christ, as he grasped it. Paul's Epistles were his chief armory. In the preface to his New Testament of 1522 he puts John's Gospel and Paul's Epistles, especially to the Romans, above Matthew, Mark, and Luke, which tell of Christ's *works*. In comparison James's Epistle is dry fodder, "eine rechte stroherne Epistel."[11] In the preface to *Romans* in the same edition, he says "Diese Epistel ist das rechte Haupstück des Neuen Testaments, und das allerlauteste Evangelium."[12] It was for him the great exposition of

8 Above, p. 69-71.

9 See generally the argumentation in *Vom Päpstthum zu Rom*, etc. (1520).

10 Letter to Spalatin, De Wette, II, p. 267. Cf. to the same, ib. II, 356.

11 ("An Epistle most decidedly composed of straw.") This preface was omitted from later editions. In the preface to James's Epistle, he said it was not the work of an Apostle.

12 ("This Epistle is the very core of the New Testament and a most illuminating Gospel.")

faith, which he thus characterizes in the same preface: "Faith is a divine work in us that changes and regenerates us as from God, and kills the old Adam, and makes us into different men . . . and brings the Holy Spirit with it."

The Psalter moved him strongly. In his Preface to it (1528) he holds it as the mirror of the Church and of the storm-tost Christian soul driven by anxiety and fear. Every soul can find apt counsel in the Psalter; can there find itself expressed: "In fine, if thou wouldst see the Holy Christian Church painted in living form and color . . . take the Psalter, and thou hast a clear pure mirror showing thee Christendom. Thou wilt also see thyself therein, and find the true 'know thyself' and God and all Creatures."

Later in life, in his *Table Talk* he says that the Psalms, St. John's Gospel and Paul's Epistles are the best to preach from when opposing heretics; but for the ordinary man and for young people, Matthew, Mark and Luke are best. Luther grasped the Scriptures very humanly, with all sides and faculties of his nature. Says he, also in his *Table Talk,* one must not attempt to weigh and understand them through our reason alone; but meditate upon them diligently with prayer. He had read the Bible through twice each year, for many years, and, as if it were a tree, had shaken each one of its branches and twigs, and every time some apples or pears had fallen to him. He felt the exhaustlessness of meaning in the Lord's Prayer.

In his address to his Augustines at Wittenberg on the *Misuse of the Mass,* Luther said, "Scripture cannot err, and who believes it cannot sin in his life." But while he held this large view of its inerrancy, and especially of its infallible presentation of the Gospel of faith, he did not hold meticulously to the inerrancy of the letter of every statement in it.

The authority of the pope was the real point at issue between Luther and the papal church. He writes of his Leipzig disputation, "if only I would not deny the power of the pope, they would readily have come to an accord with me." [13] But even he who was coming to the realization that he feared no man, felt the strain and danger of his situation. He implores the Emperor not to condemn him unheard [14] and exclaims to his friend Spalatin: "It is hard to dissent from all prelates and princes; but there is no other way to escape hell and the divine wrath." [15] After much thought and ample notice to his friends, he burnt the papal bull against him, and the Canon Law as well, before the city church of Wittenberg on the tenth of December, 1520. As he wrote to Staupitz, he did it in "trembling and prayer, but afterwards felt better over it than over any act in all my life." [16]

He was and always remained, opposed to resisting authority with arms [17]; but he had become convinced that he and every one who would be saved must fight to the last —though not with arms—against the papal laws. Through fearing no man, he stood in awe before the beliefs in which he had been educated, abandoning portions of them only under the compulsion of his reason, his conscience, and his circumstances; and still he felt anxious over what he had done, as appears in paragraphs intended to fortify the consciences of his Wittenberg Augustines placed at the beginning of his tract upon the *Misuse of the Mass*, written at the Wartburg in 1521. It is nothing that the world and all the priests of Baal dub us heretics and cry out on us, says he in substance; but we hear the cry of our own consciences, stricken with fear of God's judgment lest we be leading men astray. Even I was in doubt and fear. Could I alone be right, and all the rest of the world mistaken? Till God strengthened me, and made my heart as a rock against which the waves of apprehension beat in vain.

He had need of all his strength for his journey to

[13] To Spalatin, 1519, De Wette, I, p. 287.
[14] Jan'y, 1520. De Wette, I, p. 393.
[15] Nov., 1520, ib. I, p. 521.
[16] De Wette, I, p. 542.
[17] See e.g. to Spalatin, 1521, De Wette, I, p. 543.

Worms and his defense before the Emperor and the princes and prelates of Germany. A papal sentence, of death in this world and damnation afterwards, lay on him; and the Emperor Charles who sent him a safe-conduct commanded the burning of his books. John Huss had been burnt at Constance, whither he had gone under an emperor's safe-conduct. The Church held no faith with a condemned heretic. Luther had cause to tremble. His natural anxieties resulted in repeated illness. Yet his resolve and faith were unshaken; and he assured the Elector that he would go if he had to be carried. His journey in fact was made in a covered wagon. Cities along the route received him with acclaim. He was a hero, and the pope was hated. He writes ahead from Frankfort:

"We are coming, my Spalatin, although Satan has tried to stop me with more than one illness. All the way from Eisenach I have been ailing, and am still ailing, in ways quite new to me. And Charles's mandate [against his books], I know, has been published to frighten me. But Christ lives, and we will enter Worms in spite of all the gates of hell and powers of the air. I send a copy of the Emperor's letter. It seems best to write no more letters till, on my arrival, I see what should be done, lest we puff up Satan, whom my purpose is rather to terrify and contemn. Therefore arrange a lodging. Farewell." [18]

The papal legate, Aleander, tells of Luther's arrival at the city gates, sitting in a wagon with three companions, and protected by a hundred horsemen. As he alighted at his lodging near the Saxon Elector, he looked round with those demon eyes of his, and said "God be with me." A priest ecstatically threw his arms about him. He was soon visited by many personages, and people ran to see him. So far, in substance, Aleander.

On appearing before the Diet on the first day Luther seems to have hesitated in the presence of so august and largely hostile an assembly; but the next day he made a

18 April 14, 1521, De Wette, I, p. 586.

well ordered argument and spoke courageously in defense of his books and his convictions, to the wrath of the papal legates who protested that an excommunicated heretic had no right to defend his heresies. As for the Emperor, his face was against Luther whatever might be his own relations with the pope. For in his office Charles, equally with the pope, was heir to the Roman tradition of imperial unity. To one as to the other, Luther could only be a rebel; and the Emperor, an intense Catholic, was already started on his career of arch exterminator of heretics, in his dominions in the Low Countries, where he had the power that he lacked in German lands. He and the papal party would quickly have put an end to Luther's words and life, if Luther had not had the protection of the Saxon Elector and the support of a large proportion of all classes in Germany.

In spite of commands, exhortations and persuasion, within the Diet and without, Luther refused to recant, or materially to retract his statements. He left Worms as he had entered it, an excommunicated heretic. The Emperor's ban followed quickly, proclaiming him an outlaw. But from these cumulative dangers he was spirited away, out of the sight and ken of enemies and friends alike, to a benignant confinement at the Wartburg, the historic castle, then belonging to the Saxon Elector. There he stayed for eight months, translating the New Testament, writing letters and tracts to exhort trembling or over-zealous friends, fighting the devil as well as mortal enemies, and advancing in his faith from strength to strength.

It was irksome to be confined, and bodily withheld from the strife. Half humorously, half lugubriously, Luther dates his letters, "in the region of the birds," "on my Patmos," "from my hermitage." Vehemently he works; or, again, the perturbations of his soul and body prostrate his energies. "Now for a week, I do neither write, nor pray, nor study, vexed with temptations of the flesh and other ills," he writes Melanchthon.[19] His words had already be-

19 De Wette, II, p. 22.

come a power with his friends, a terror to others. Albrecht, archbishop of Mainz, to relieve whose impecuniousness Tetzel had sold indulgences, now bethought him to do a little business quietly in that line at Halle. The Elector had no wish to make an enemy of the princely primate of Germany, and knowing that Luther was breathing forth threatenings, asked him to keep silence. Neither then, nor ever afterwards, did Luther hold his peace when speech was called for; and the vigor of his threats of public attack, made in a private letter to the archbishop,[20] caused the latter to stop the sale and excuse himself to Luther in a letter.

In fact while at the Wartburg, as before and afterwards through his life, Luther worked and wrote torrentially. There were years when his productions monopolized the presses of Germany. At the Wartburg he seems first to have completed a little writing which showed how dearly he still loved the teachings and traditions of the Church. It was a charming piece for the Elector, *On the Song of Praise of the holy Virgin Mary, called the Magnificat.* He honors her sinlessness, and almost prays to her, saying at the beginning, "May the same gentle Mother procure me the spirit to interpret her song aright," and at the end, "This may Christ grant us through the intercession of his dear Mother Mary."

Paying this tribute to the clinging sentiments of religious habit, Luther proceeded none the less manfully to disembarrass his mind of matters which more loudly demanded discarding. He wrote a tract *On the power of the pope to compel Confession,* which he sent with an inspiring letter to a doughty patron and protector of his, the great swashbuckler knight Von Sickingen.[21] He then took up the marriage of priests, on which Carlstadt and Melanchthon had already taken a radical stand. Luther fundamentally agreeing with them, still wished to test their grounds more

20 De Wette, II, pp. 112-114. So Luther did not publish his *Against the Idol at Halle.*
21 De Wette, II, 13.

thoroughly. Next he undertook to settle the burning question whether monastic vows were binding. He sent his *Opinion* to his own father, who had so bitterly opposed his purpose to become a monk, and with it a telling letter,[22] in which he recalls the anxieties and the sudden fear that drove him into the convent, and his father's doubt whether it was not a crazed delusion:—and now, dear father, "wilt thou still drag me out? For still art thou father, and I am son, and all vows mean nothing. . . . But the Lord has forestalled thee, and has himself delivered me. For what signifies it, whether I wear the cowl or lay it off? Cowl and tonsure do not make the monk. 'All is yours,' says Paul, 'and you are Christ's'; and why should I be the cowl's and not the cowl rather be mine? My conscience has become free, which means that I have become free. So I am a monk and yet no monk, a new creature, not the pope's, but Christ's." Satan foresaw what great scathe he was to suffer from me, and attempted my ruin. But from this book "thou mayest see through what signs and wonders Christ has loosed me from the monk's vow and given me such freedom that, while he has made me the servant of all, I am subject to none but him alone. For he is my bishop, directly over me, my abbot, prior, lord, father and teacher. Henceforth I recognize none other."

In this tract, which was written in Latin, Luther maintains that the monk's vow is opposed to God and scripture; for whatever goes beyond the words of Christ is man's invention. To turn that which was at most a counsel in the Gospel into a command, is to go beyond and against the Gospel. The monastic vow is opposed to faith, and to the freedom wherein faith makes us free from all things. It infringes the gospel freedom set by God, which is no less a sin than to break any other commandment. It is opposed to love of neighbor, to obedience to parents, and to natural reason. "Those who make their vows intending

22 De Wette, II, 100 sqq.—also printed as a preface to Luther's *Urtheil über die Mönchsgelübde*.

to become good and blessed through this way of life, to blot out their sins and gain riches through good works, are as godless Jews fallen from faith."

At the same time Luther made ready another tract, *On the Misuse of the Mass*, from which certain opening reflections have already been taken. It presented Luther's conception of the priesthood and the sacrament of the body and blood of Christ, maintaining that this sacrament is not a sacrifice offered to God in propitiation for our sins, but is received from Him in token of His free forgiveness. There is one priest, who is Christ; the New Testament ordains no visible priesthood beside him; but all Christians are priests with Christ. Consequently the papal priesthood is nothing, their acts and laws are nothing; and the Mass which they call a sacrifice is sheer idolatry, a fabrication added to God's Testament.

It is hard for weak consciences to think that so many people have been damned in this idolatry, despite all the churches and cloisters where myriad daily masses are said; and they are tempted to believe the mass is instituted by God because it has been instituted by the Church. But the Church did not institute it, since the Church ordains nothing beyond God's word; and whatever body makes the attempt is no Church. Let us have done with the pope's priesthood and their mass; and to the argument that ordained power has authority to command, make reply: Go and take counsel with the blasphemers of those Gomorrahs, Paris and Louvain; we maintain with the power of the Gospel, that when ye rule without God's word, ye are the devil's priests, and your office and priesthood is the work of the devil to crush out the Spirit and Word of God.

The time was at hand when Luther no longer could endure to write and fight from his retreat. Disturbances among his own Wittenbergers demanded his presence and his voice. His more radically minded followers—whom Luther declared hurt him more than all his enemies and all the devils too [23]—had rudely gone to work; and fana-

23 De Wette, II, p. 165.

tics were come from Zwickau, who would overthrow all things. Wittenberg was becoming a scandal; the town council petitioned him to return. The Elector, himself troubled by many thorny questions, felt still greater anxiety lest Luther's return should embroil him with the Emperor and endanger the reformer's life: demands would be made for his surrender, to his certain death. So at least it seemed to the Elector, and he wrote asking Luther not to come. Luther did not tarry at the Wartburg to reply, but answered from the road to Wittenberg. His letter respectfully explained the urgency of the situation, and then proceeded: "As for my own fate, most gracious Lord, I answer thus: Your Electoral Grace knows, or if not, will be informed by this, that I have received the Gospel not from men, but solely from Heaven, through our Lord Jesus Christ, and well might and henceforth will declare and subscribe myself a servant and evangelist. If I have submitted to be heard and judged, it has been through no doubt of this, but from over-humility in order to win others. Now I see my humility bringing the Gospel into contempt, and that the devil will take the whole place, where I intended to give him but a palm; so my conscience compels me to act otherwise."

"I have done enough for your Electoral Grace by retiring for a year, obediently. For the devil knows that I have not done this from cowardice. He saw it in my heart, as I entered Worms, that had there been as many devils there as tiles on the roofs, I would have sprung into their midst gladly. Duke George [24] is not the equal of a single devil. And since the Father of all mercies has through his Gospel made us glad lords over all the devils and death, so that we may call him our own dear Father, your Grace will see what shame we should put on Him if we did not trust Him to make us lords over the anger of Duke George. . . .

[24] Duke George, ruler over the other parts of Saxony, an earnest Catholic, and Luther's enemy.

"These things I have written to your Grace so that your Grace may know that I come to Wittenberg under a higher guard than that of the Prince Elector. Nor do I propose to seek that protection of your Electoral Grace. Rather it is I that would protect you. Indeed if I knew that your Grace could and would protect me, I would not come. In this business the sword should not and cannot either advise or aid; God must do all by Himself. Therefore he who has most faith will best protect. And since I perceive your Electoral Grace to be still weak in faith, I cannot find in you the man who could protect or save me."

The letter proceeds further to absolve the Elector from responsibility for Luther's safety; and begs him not to oppose the carrying out of any imperial edict. For himself, Christ has not so taught him that he should be a burden to another Christian. "Herewith I commend your princely Electoral Grace to the grace of God. . . . If your Grace believed, you would see the glory of God; since you do not yet believe, you have seen nothing." [25]

So Luther made his way to Wittenberg. The Elector, better than his protest, continued his protection. If Luther's word had first unchained the tempest which so rudely was throwing down the old forms and ceremonies of worship, his word and presence now restored peace. Mightily had he grasped for himself, and set forth for others, Paul's great doctrine of justification by faith. Now with equal power and effect he set forth another side of the great apostle's teaching, that it is not the Christian's part to cause his weaker brother to stumble. He preached sermons on eight successive days, and cast a spell of order and toleration over the city.

In the first sermon he pointed out to his hearers, who thronged the large city church, that each Christian must

---

[25] This, perhaps the most famous of all Luther's letters, is printed in De Wette, II, 137 sqq., and elsewhere very often.

answer and fight for himself against the devil and death. Each should know the tenets of his faith. We are all children of wrath; our acts and thoughts are sinful and as nothing in the sight of God. But God gave his Son; and at this point the preacher briefly recalled the substance of Christ's gospel. To benefit by it faith is needed; then love of one another, in which his auditors seemed to have failed. Patience also is required, and forbearance. Each shall not insist upon his own way, but yield so as to win those who are without. No one should so use his freedom as to give offence to those who are weak in faith. You have surely the pure word of God; act then soberly and considerately. Our warfare is with the devil, who has many wiles. Those have erred who have inconsiderately swept away the mass, without advising with me—with me, who was called to preach, not by my will, but against it. Suppose your taunts to have driven some brother, against his conscience, to eat meat on Friday, and in the hour of death he is seized with fear;—on whose head falls the blame?

So speaks Luther's broad human and Pauline forbearance. His rock-ribbed intolerance will elsewhere strike us. The second sermon opens with the avowal that the popish sacrificial mass is an abomination; but it is not for us to tear it out by the hair; leave it to God. Why? Because *I* do not hold men's hearts as clay in my hand; I can speak to the ear, but cannot force my words into their hearts. Let our words work free; but use no force. We preach the truth; let that work. Paul came to Athens, and saw the altars of idolatry. Did he rush to kick them over with his foot? Let faith be free. I will preach against the mass; but will not cast it out by force. I spoke against indulgences, gently, with the word of God, raising no tumult; and so I weakened the papacy more than the Kaiser ever did. Blood might have been poured out, had I done differently.

Monks' vows are null, affirms the next sermon; as null as if I had vowed to strike my father in the face. Yet to hurry out of convents and marry, is not yet for all. It should be left to the conscience of each. So images are useless; but do ye leave each man free to keep or reject them. Only one must not pray to them. Let us preach that images are vanities, but that no outer thing can injure faith.

The remaining sermons consider points of contention: taking the Sacrament into the communicant's hands; insistence upon both the bread and wine; the question of confession. Also the fruit of the Sacrament which is love.

The incidents of Luther's life so far referred to, with his words and writings, tempt us to further efforts to place him in proper categories of appreciation and form some estimate of him. At all events, he calls for emphatic statements. One must not approach him mincingly, nor be overnice. To be misled or repelled by certain of his qualities would be to hesitate over the immaterial and tarry with the impertinent. If we find contradictions in the man as well as in his doctrines, we should seek their harmony in the reaches of his nature and the reasonings which there had their home. We may find the contradictions bound together, as by the grace of God, into a mighty personality speaking always to one high argument.

In a letter to Melanchthon,[26] Luther says that his opponents to show their smartness gather contradictions from his books. "How can those asses judge the contradictions in our doctrine, who understand neither of the contradictories? For what else can our doctrines be in the eyes of the wicked than sheer contradiction, since it both requires and condemns works, abolishes and restores ritual, honors and reproves the magistrates, asserts and denies sin?"

"I am a peasant's son," says Luther, "my father, grandfather, and forebears, were *echte Bauern*. My father when young was a poor miner; my mother carried the wood on her back: and so they brought us up." Luther was a peasant too. The rank and ready coarseness of the peasant was an obvious element of his nature to the end. It crops out through his talk and writing in language absolutely un-

26 July, 1530, De Wette, IV, p. 103.

quotable even for purposes of illustration. It should not be compared with the expressions of many an Italian humanist; for such men were themselves contaminate, while Luther's soul, even as his life, was pure. A juster comparison lies with the great-natured Rabelais; but the latter's obscenity is a thing of imaginative art. Luther's coarseness is never for its own sake. Sudden, and uncalled for as it sometimes seems to us, it was with him a natural mode of speech, the ready weapon of anger and denunciation.

For Luther was a man of wrath, of violent and cyclopean indignation. He did not restrain it; but poured it out on the offense, as the wrath of God, given him to deliver. If he felt that the occasion called for tolerance and love, he was persuasive and compelling in these qualities, as when he calmed the Wittenberg disorders. But anger naturally nerved him to combat; he says in his *Table Talk* that people had warned him at the outset not to attack the pope: "but when I was angry, I went at it like a blindfold horse." That was human or animal; but he was also convinced of the divine sanction of his wrath: "The anger of my mouth is not my anger, but God's anger," he cried to a papal legate. And there could not be enough of it. "I have never satisfied myself and the enormousness of my anger against the papal monster; nor do I think I shall ever be able to satisfy it." [27] Luther was a German, and understood the gospel of hate as well as love.[28] As the years passed, neither his hate nor his language became mollified. In his tract of 1545, *Against the Roman papacy founded by the devil,* the pope instead of the allerheiligster (most holy) has become the allerhöllischte (most hellish) father, Sanctus Paulus Tertius. That pope, forsooth, has

[27] Aug., 1545, De Wette, V, p. 754.
[28] It seems to me that in spirit the recent German war harks back to Luther, even to his tract upon the Freedom of a Christian man: each man outwardly subject to the powers that be, bounden in outward obedience; but inwardly free, and even finding in his inward freedom a certain detachment from responsibility for the nature of his outward acts, commanded by the powers that be.

written to the Kaiser, angrily maintaining that the pope alone may call a council—which shall meet at Trent. Against such a council, whose decrees may be given, changed or nullified by the "abominable abomination at Rome calling himself the pope," Luther protests with vigorous wrath, addressing the pope always as "your hellishness." "*I* mock the pope!" he exclaims. "Good God, I am too slight a thing to mock that which has mocked the world to its perdition for six hundred years."

His convinced wrath was directed not only against Rome and her partisans; but against any one whom he thought was falsifying God's doctrine. "My one sole glory," he writes to Melanchthon, "is that I have delivered the pure and unadulterated word of God. . . . I believe that Zwingli is deserving of holy hate for his obstinate wickedness against the holy word of God." [29] Thus he delivered himself because of the Swiss reformer's view of the Sacrament of the Lord's Supper. Luther abominated transubstantiation; but on no point of doctrine did he insist more violently than on the real presence of the body and blood of Christ. This was the rock of controversy on which he and Zwingli wrecked the cause of Protestant unity two years later, at the Marburg colloquy, when Luther sat him at the conference table and wrote on it in chalk the words "This is my body,"—from which he would not swerve. He and Zwingli reached an agreement on other points; but on this they parted.

The German Bucer, an early admirer of Luther, who was destined to carry on so excellently the work of the Reform at Strassburg, held views like Zwingli's. Having him in mind, Luther wrote: "Satan is angry, and perhaps feels that the Day of Christ is at hand. Therefore he rages so cruelly and will deprive us of the Saviour Jesus Christ through his trickery. Under the papacy he was sheer flesh, making out that even monks' cowls were holy. Now will

29 Oct., 1527, De Wette, III, 215.

he be sheer spirit, making out that the flesh and word of Christ are nothing." [30]

The vehemence of Luther's speech, the violence of his convictions, alike were needed for the doing of the work he did. Millions of protests had been wasted on the mighty mammon of the Church. Soft words and gentle persuasions would still have been futile. Even the rapier satire of Erasmus did not pierce the monster. No reform could be achieved by anyone so long as the authority of the pope remained unimpeached, and the unity of the Roman Catholic Church unbroken. Vituperation, revolt, attack, were needed. It may be, as men have thought, that Luther's breach with Rome not only underlay the spiritual remaking of the lands which became Protestant, but compelled the Roman Catholic Church to redeem itself from its overgrowth of abuse and corruption.

One may also argue for the need of Luther's firm, not to say violent, insistence upon certain doctrines, that of the Real Presence, for example. For the man was preaching no Erasmian piety, or ethics, of the obvious rational type, which men might accept and remain unmoved. He was preaching religion; he was delivering doctrine, not rationalism, to his followers: the doctrines which he held to be those of the true Christian faith and necessary for salvation. "Men still doubt that my preaching is God's word: that the true body and blood of Christ is received in the Sacrament, or that in baptism sins are washed away by the blood of Christ. But that I teach and preach the veritable word of God, I will pledge my soul and will die for it. . . . If thou believest this thou art blessed; if thou dost not, thou art damned." *(Table Talk.)*

The Protestant religion needed to be as stiff and staunch in doctrine as the Catholic, and as imperative. The world was not yet interested in liberalism and tolerance. It wanted sure salvation. Luther fought for and established his way of salvation, and disproved the Roman

[30] De Wette, III, 206

system, showed its falsity, its inefficiency. He who followed the Roman way would be damned just as surely, according to the Lutheran conviction, as in Catholic eyes men would be damned for following Luther. Who would have cared for Luther's faith had he taught or admitted that men could just as well be saved in the bosom of the Catholic Church? It did not irk Luther and his followers, any more than it did the Calvinists or the Catholics, or the Mohammedans for that matter, to think of many damned.

Luther wrote a book of *Fourteen Consolations for the Downcast and Oppressed,* and more especially for the Elector, sick and weary in the year 1519. In this work of reasonable Christian comfort, after reviewing the ills of life and the pains of hell, he remarks: "How many thousand are in hell's eternal damnation who have scarcely a thousandth part of our sins? How many young girls and boys are there, and, as we say, 'innocent children'? How many monks, priests, married people, who seemed to serve God all their lives, and now are eternally punished perhaps for a single sin? For . . . the same justice of God does its office on each sin, hating and damning it in whomsoever found." So, argues Luther, we realize the boundless pity of God in not damning us, and may well be thankful. He agrees with Augustine that he would not willingly live his life again, with its pains and anxieties. He speaks of the seven ills and seven compensations, or *goods,* such as a glad heart, and the goods of the mind, the sense of the glory of God, and the good things promised us through Christ hereafter, which include satisfaction from the punishment of sin in the damned, while through love we make the joys and sorrows of the saints our own.

Wonderful have been human consolations and convictions! Without earnest, sincere, terrible convictions the world might have stayed still; they are also among the plagues which have fallen upon men, driving those obsessed by them to blood and pious rapine.

So many elements, so many potent antecedents came to effective combination and living actuality in Luther. In the vortex of his nature, the *vivida vis* of living life made them all to live again. He was altogether alive, and put life into whatever he thought or said or wrote. His personality lives in every sentence, one is tempted to say, from the beginning to the end at last of the enormous array of his writings. He was a superman in power, in energy, in fertile facility. His reason does not work alone, nor does he ever act by impulse merely: his faculties act together spontaneously—with a spontaneity not always calculable for other men. No man was like him. Not another one of the reformers in his time or after him was spontaneous and alive as Luther was alive, not Zwingli, not Calvin.

The strength of Luther's faith, and the firm and violent convictions of which we have been speaking, owed something to his aliveness and vital imagination, and to his sensitive perception and realization of the intimacies of life about him, and the immeasurable reaches of existence which were as assured as the stars above his head. If Duke George was not the equal of a single devil, what was he then compared with the power of God shown in the rose which Luther holds in his hand, while he wonders at God's workmanship in the budding of trees in the spring, and in the functions of the human body. Consciousness of nature's marvels is a stay and comfort in times of trial, and how surely such for one who knows them to be creatures of Him who holds alike the faithful man and all his enemies in the hollow of His hand! Luther likewise loved his own children intimately and imaginatively. He saw them as God's best gifts, and let his mind play around their child natures, so ready for love and faith. Such love of children is another stay and comfort.

Wonderful illustrations of the calm and happy assurance thus given him lie in letters written from the Elector's castle of Coburg in the year 1530. It was an anxious time. The imperial diet was sitting at Augsburg, with the hostile Emperor at its head. The Saxon Elector John [31] was there,

---

[31] Who had succeeded the Elector Frederick in 1525.

with Melanchthon and other theologians, who were to draw up the presentation of their faith known as the Augsburg Confession. But Luther was left at Coburg, a hundred and thirty miles away, on the Saxon border. Being under the imperial ban, he could not appear before the Emperor; and his presence would have excited animosity when the Lutherans desired concord. So Luther abode those anxious months at Coburg, while others fought the fight that was his. A restless, anxious state was that of this sequestered leader, restricted to reports of the battle, and to his letters of exhortation and admonishment in return. As all men knew, he would have yielded nothing, and could not have tipped his speech with velvet, or "walked as softly" as Melanchthon. He approved of the "Confession," if only they would leave off dallying with compromises and quit the diet. Quivering with impatience, he writes to them in July to leave, since they had spoken: "Igitur absolvo vos in nomine Domini ab isto conventu. Immer wieder heim, immer heim!!" [32] Constantly and most directly, he comforts himself with his trust in God, for himself and for his cause, as we read in many a letter to Melanchthon and to others. He assures Melanchthon that the troubles which seem to master the latter are huge only through his lack of faith. It is his learning that bothers him—as if anything could be accomplished through useless solicitudes. He is his own direct foe, armed by the devil against himself. "Christ died once for our sins, but for justice and truth he does not die, but lives and reigns. If this is true, what fear then for the truth, if he reigns? But, do you say, it will be overthrown by the anger of God? Let us be overthrown with it, but not through ourselves." [33] And again: "If we shall fall, Christ falls with us, to wit, he, the ruler of the world! So be it: if he shall fall, I had rather fall with Christ

[32] ("Therefore in the name of the Lord, I absolve you from this diet. Home! Ever home again!!") De Wette, IV, 96. Luther often mingles Latin and German in his letters, as the one or the other tongue best expresses him.

[33] June 27, 1530, De Wette, IV, p. 49.

than stand with Caesar." [34] Later in the summer, he writes comforting a certain Jonas: "Gratiam et pacem in Christo. Ego, mi Jonas, nostram causam Christo commendavi serio (earnestly), et is promisit mihi . . . suam hanc causam esse et fore: [35] *And he has promised me that our cause is His and shall be!"*

Such were his direct self-heartenings. The more subtle serenity reflected in his mind from God's creation is illustrated by a letter written in lighter vein to those who lived with him at Wittenberg:

"To my dear table-companions, Peter and Jerome Weller, and Henry Schneidewin, and others at Wittenberg, severally and jointly: Grace and peace in Christ Jesus, dear sirs and friends. I have received the letter you all wrote and have learned how everything is going. That you may hear in turn how we are doing, I would have you know that we, namely, I, Master Veit, and Cyriac, did not go to the diet at Augsburg, but have come to another diet instead.

"There is a grove just under our windows like a small forest. There the jackdaws and crows are holding a diet. They ride in and out, and keep up a racket day and night without ceasing, as if they were all crazy-drunk. Young and old chatter together in such a fashion that I wonder voice and breath hold out. I should like to know whether there are any such knights and warriors still left with you. It seems as if they must have gathered here from all the world.

"I have not yet seen their emperor; but the nobility and bigwigs constantly flit and gad about before our eyes, not very expensively clothed, but simply, in one

34 June 30, 1530, ib. p. 62.
35 De Wette, IV, p. 157. I leave this sentence in the Latin. Luther's Latin letters are as direct and forcible as his German. Perhaps he never wrote a finer body of letters than those written from Coburg, from April to October, 1530. They make the first two hundred pages of De Wette's fourth volume.

color, all alike black, and all alike gray-eyed. They all
sing the same song, but there is an agreeable contrast
between young and old, great and small. They care
nothing for grand palaces and halls, for their hall is
vaulted with the beautiful, broad sky, its floor is paved
with lovely green branches, and its wall are as wide as
the world. They do not ask for horses or armor; they
have feathered chariots to escape the hunters. They
are high and mighty lords, but I don't yet know what
they are deciding. So far as I have been able to learn
from an interpreter, they plan a great war against wheat,
barley, oats, malt, and all sorts of grain, and many a
one will show himself a hero and do valiant deeds.

"So we sit here in the diet, listening and looking on
with great pleasure, as the princes and lords with the
other estates of the realm so merrily sing and feast.
It gives us special delight to see in how knightly a fashion they strut about, polish their bills, and fall upon
the defense that they may conquer and acquit themselves honorably against corn and malt. We wish them
fortune and health, that they may all be impaled on a
spit together.

"Methinks they are none other than the sophists
and papists with their preaching and writing. All of
them I must have in a crowd before me that I may hear
their lovely voices and sermons, and see how useful a
tribe they are, destroying everything on earth, and for
a change chattering to kill time.

"To-day we heard the first nightingale, for she was
afraid to trust our April. We have had lovely weather
and no rain except a little yesterday. It is perhaps otherwise with you. God bless you! Take good care of the
house.

"From the *Diet of the Malt-Robbers,* April 28, 1530.
MARTIN LUTHER, *Doctor.*" [36]

[36] I have taken this translation from the excellent book of A. C.
McGiffert, *Martin Luther, the Man and his Work.* The original
is in De Wette, IV, p. 8. Luther was so amused with his idea of
a Reichstag (diet) of rooks and daws, that he repeated it in
several letters.

Two or three months later Luther wrote to Brück, the Elector's chancellor, a letter of wonderful comforting indicative of the peace which he drew from the sublimities of nature. He speaks of anxieties common to them both, and his trust in God who listens to their prayers, and will forget them never, and then says:

"I have lately seen two miracles. I looked out of the window, I saw the stars in heaven and the whole great vault of God, and saw nowhere any pillars on which the Master had set it. Yet the heavens fell not, and the vault stands fast. Now there are some who look for such pillars, and gladly would feel and grasp them. Because they cannot, they worry and tremble, as if the heavens would fall in, just because they cannot see and grasp the pillars. If they could grasp them, the heaven would stand fast!

"Again, I saw great thick clouds sweeping over us, so heavy that they seemed like a great sea; and I saw no footing for them and nothing to constrain them. Yet they did not fall on us, but greeted us with a sour face, and flew away. When they were gone the rainbow shone forth, as floor and roof, above us, which had held them—a weak thin little floor and roof, vanishing in the clouds, and more like a ray shining through painted glass than a strong floor. . . . Yet it upheld the weight of water and protected us. Still there are those who fearfully regard the weight of the cloud masses, rather than this thin small ray. They would gladly feel and make sure of its strength, and since they cannot, they fear that the clouds will bring an eternal Deluge (Sündfluth).

"So much I write to your Honor in friendly jest, and yet not in jest; since I learn with joy of your Honor's steadfast and trustful courage in this our trial. I had hoped that at least political peace could be maintained; but God's thoughts are above ours . . . and if He were to grant us peace from the Kaiser, the Kaiser and not

He might have the glory. . . . Our rainbow is weak; their [the enemies'] clouds are mighty; but in the end it will appear whose is the thunderbolt." [37]

But there were catastrophes in Luther's life more dire than any arising from the attack of enemies. Against direct attack his courage was invincible and his faith a shield. The tragedies of his life were those conditions or events which seemed to show the futility or the evil results of what he had taught and worked for. Among such positive ill results from Luther's point of view might be set the obstreperous spiritual anarchy, as of Zwickau prophets and Anabaptists, which went so far beyond the orderly conservative religious revolution that was Luther's plan. Yet his enemies alleged, and Luther feared, that the fervor of his own teachings had loosed the misguided energies and entered the abominable opinions of intellectual radicals like Carlstadt and fanatic anarchists like Münzer.

Carlstadt was a keenly reasoning, radically minded man. He had been Luther's associate in the Leipzig debate against Eck in 1521. But while Luther was in the Wartburg, Carlstadt became moved with desire to set aside every religious practice and convention for which he could not find direct authority in Scripture. He was as radical in handling Holy Writ, and disposed to attack everybody's prejudices and acceptances in his insistence upon his new evangelical way of living and worshipping. Luther had become to him a time-server and a tyrant; while on his part he became an active thorn in Luther's flesh. Münzer was an evangelical anarchist, preaching the Gospel of God's fiery word resounding within the individual soul. Its dictates were to be made good not merely by persuasion, but with fire and sword, as Münzer demonstrated by taking up the peasants' cause, and urging them to blood. He was akin to the Anabaptists, as various anarchistic sects were called who were for throwing down

[37] Aug., 1530, De Wette, IV, 127 sqq.

the social structure altogether, and agreed in little beyond denying the validity of infant baptism and demanding adult immersion, for the full cleansing of sin. They too took to the sword, and largely perished by it too, when the forces of the established order, as well as the power of religious intolerance, were driven against them. But they spread far and wide in the sixteenth century, in Germany, the Low Countries, Switzerland, even France; the proper Lutherans in Germany were just as anxious as Calvin and the French adherents of the Reform, to clear their skirts of all connection with the Anabaptist anarchy.

The Peasants' War (1525-6) was worst of all. Its distressful causes broke out repeatedly in blood before Luther's day. But now unquestionably his doctrine of Christian liberty was bearing fruit beyond his purpose and intent. Relief from oppression was the spiritual freedom which the peasants sought, and formulated in their Articles. These seem to us quite reasonable, but in 1525 they meant drastic change. The harsh rejection of them by the princes, the bloody dispersal of the peasants' gatherings, aroused fiercer passions in the sufferers, and drew Münzer and other preachers into a joint tumultuous movement for a manhood equality set on the prior massacre of magistrates and rulers. Of course Luther was appealed to, and his writings quoted, to support these aims. His first reply was *An Exhortation to Peace, in response to the Twelve Articles of the Swabian Peasants*. He admonished them to present their grievances in an orderly and peaceful way, and reminded the princes too that there had been injustice and oppression to justify the peasants' discontent. But he was staunch against mob violence, maintaining, as he always maintained, that the rulers alone could use the sword divinely committed to them. Let not the peasants invoke Christ's Gospel which had not to do with such affairs. If they were followers of Christ, they would drop their arms and take to prayer. Earthly society is built on inequalities; the Christian's liberty touches them not, but exists and serves in the midst of them.

Thus Luther was on the side of Christian freedom and the divine authority of rulers. He had spoken moderately, so far, but the outrages and riots witnessed by him soon after, and the appeal to his teaching to justify them, drove him mad. In his pamphlet, *Against the Murderous and Robbing Mobs of Peasants,* he turned on them with fury. He likened them to mad dogs; all the devils of hell must have entered into them. He urged the princes not to hesitate for conscience's sake, but to slay them without mercy; if a ruler fighting in this war himself was slain, it was a martyr's death.

Luther was a peasant's son; yet, before this insurrection, he held a low opinion of the common man's intelligence. The spiritual disturbance, which outran so wildly the respectability of his own reforms, confirmed his contempt for the common people who were led so easily beyond decency and reason and the correct understanding of Christ's Gospel. He expressed this contempt in his diatribe, *Against the heavenly prophets* (1524-1525), saying that the Common herd—*Herr Omnes*—must be made to behave by the sword and the constraint of law, as wild beasts are held in chains and cages. Although Luther was the most steadfast of men, and with a mighty faith in God, he and his reformed religion were in fact protected and preserved by the favor of the princely rulers of the land. In return, Luther and his state-protected Church were on the side of law and order and authority; and the spokesmen of that church, even though unconsciously, were influenced by social and political considerations.

As was shown in the matter of the fatal bigamy of Landgrave Philip of Hesse. The political fortunes of Lutheran Protestantism were at their zenith in 1540 when Philip, the ablest of the Protestant princes, feeling a resistless desire to marry a lady-in-waiting, wedded her secretly, but with the consent of his still living though not in all respects satisfactory consort. It was bigamy, and a crime by the laws of the Empire. The Landgrave appealed to Luther and Melanchthon to assuage his conscience, for he was a zealous Protestant, and had long felt qualms at the immoralities to which the vigor of his body impelled him.

Before this, the example of the Patriarchs had led some of the Anabaptists to declare for polygamy. Luther himself said in his *Babylonian Captivity of the Church* that bigamy was better than divorce. He had elsewhere written that he found no Scripture authority barring plurality of wives, but he hoped the custom would not be introduced among Christians; and some years before 1540 he so advised the Landgrave. But now moved by the Landgrave's urgent appeal and presentation of his scruples, Luther, Melanchthon and Bucer formally excused and sanctioned his bigamy, but as an exceptional case, not to be made a precedent, and if possible to be kept a secret.

This weak and baneful decision brought discredit and disaster on the Protestants. In connection, however, with this failure of Luther in firmness and foresight, one may add that he was a man by nature sympathetic with the stress of bodily desire. His own life was absolutely free from reproach, save, of course, that his marriage was a deadly sin in Catholic eyes. He was forty-two years old in 1525 when it took place; and if he was moved by natural need and impulse, he had given long and earnest doctrinal consideration to the question, and for several years had held all men free to marry or abstain. There is no evidence that personal desire to marry influenced his acts or doctrines. When he did marry, he made a faithful husband and a loving father. He was also a true lover of his friends, a hater of his enemies. His speech was mostly of religion; but he could be a jovial companion, eating and drinking like a German, and delighting in song.

To the Peasants' War and the Landgrave's bigamy, events which proved so tragic for the life and work of Luther, may be added disappointment over the result of his teaching and great labors. He had held high hopes that when men had been shown the Gospel truth, and accepted it, their lives would correspond; and there would be a regeneration of the nation. None such took place. Lutherans remained much as they had been before; while through Lutheran lands worship and education deteriorated, because the old compulsory ordinances were weakened or disturbed, and men were slack and negligent.

Luther declared that had he foreseen the toil and danger to come to him, wild horses would not have dragged him into the struggle. He had thought men sinned from ignorance, and only needed to be shown the right way! He had not supposed that the world would continue evil, when the true gospel had been preached. He had no idea how men, especially the clergy, despised God's Word in their hearts. Before the gospel was preached, men's hearts were hidden. Christ is the revealer of hearts; and now we know that princes, bishops, nobles, burghers, peasants, all are a lot of devils!

So Luther spoke in disappointment and depression. A little over a year before his death, when plagued by the course of events, by sickness in his family and his own bodily ills, he writes to a friend from out of even blacker depths: "Grace and peace in the Lord. I write briefly, my Jacob, lest I should write nothing at all, as if forgetful of thee. I am dull, tired, feeble, a useless old man. I have finished my course; it remains that the Lord should gather me to my fathers, and that worms and corruption should have their due. I have lived enough, if it is to be called life. Do thou pray for me, that the hour of my passing may be pleasing to God and salutary to myself. I care nothing for Caesar and the whole empire, except to commend them in my prayers to God. The world also seems to me to have come to the hour of its passing away, and to have waxed old like a garment, as the Psalm says, and soon to suffer change. Amen. There is no heroic virtue left in the princes, but only incurable hatred and dissension, avarice and the cupidity of profit. So the State is without strength, and the head runs the full course of Isaiah third. Wherefore no good can be hoped for, unless that the day of the glory of the great God and our redemption be revealed." [38]

But Luther had always assaulted vigorously those evils which were the chief ground of his depression. Thus in October, 1525, he informed the new Elector John of the wretched state of the parish priests: "No one gives, no one pays. Offerings have ceased, and parish incomes diminished. The common man has no regard for either preacher or pastor. Unless your Electoral Grace establishes order and support for them, the clergy will have no homes, and there will be neither schools nor scholars; and God's Word and service will fall to the ground." [39]

The Elector appointed a commission to visit the parishes and take action. There was need. For if the Roman clergy, as Luther said, had shamefully neglected church worship and religious instruction, the condition of the churches had since become worse, especially in the country, where the peasants seemed to have lost all religion. Gradually, however, as may be read, the tide of demoralization was checked in Saxony; and following the example of the Elector, the Lutheran princes of Germany established reformed state churches in their domains, conserving as much as seemed feasible of the old ecclesiastical order.[40]

Sometime after returning from his visitation of the Saxon churches, Luther composed the *Shorter* and the *Longer* catechisms to remedy the ignorance of pastors as well as flocks. Catholic primers existed, as well as manuals of preparation for confession and the Communion.[41] These may have afforded him suggestion. But in his hands and under his direction the Catechism became a most

38 To Jacob Probst, Dec., 1544, De Wette, V, p. 7703.
39 Oct. 31, 1525, De Wette, III, p. 39.
40 See chap. XXI. of McGiffert's *Martin Luther*.
41 See Jannsen, *Ges. des deutschen Volkes*, I, pp. 46 sqq. (18th edition).

important means of instruction in the Lutheran faith, as well as an expository declaration of its principles and substance. The *Shorter Catechism* opened with an exhortation to pastors and preachers and a cry to God: Hilf! lieber Gott! in this ignorance so abominable that many pastors do not know the Lord's Prayer or the Creed or the Ten Commandments. The pastors were then instructed as to their duties, and admonished that those among their flocks who refused to learn should be kept from the land. Afterwards comes the substance of the Catechism, that which every good householder should impress upon his household. The Ten Commandments are given and briefly and piously explained; likewise the Apostles' Creed and the Lord's Prayer, in telling words. Next a brief explanation of the sacraments of baptism and the communion; also short forms of confession, of private prayer and grace at table; and forms for pastors to use in marrying and baptising.

The *Longer Catechism* expands the matter. Great stress is laid upon the Ten Commandments, which are so taken and expounded as to include the compass of Christian piety. "So we have the Ten Commandments as a pattern of the divine doctrine, what we shall do that our whole life be pleasing to God, and the true spring and conduit in which must flow everything that is to be a good work: so that beyond the Ten Commandments no work or thing can be good and pleasing to God, however great and precious it may be before the world." The Creed, the Lord's Prayer, the sacraments of baptism and communion, with other matters, are then given with lengthy comment. These two Catechisms became the vehicle of Christian instruction in the Lutheran churches, a function likewise to be fulfilled by Calvin's Catechisms in the churches following the Geneva Reform.

Luther likewise energetically met the need to re-establish education, in the tract *To the Burgermasters and Councillors of the Cities,* written in 1524. He speaks of the general admission that in German lands the high-schools are declining and the convent schools falling to pieces:—well enough that the latter should go down and that people should refuse to send their children to such nests of the devil. Now, raging at the fall of convents, where he was wont to trap young souls, he aims at the destruction of all schools, to the further ensnaring of the young. Alas! men give gulden for the war against the Turks, but do not see that they should give a hundred times as much to make their children Christians. I beg you, dear friends, to realize how much it profits Christ and all of us, to help the young.

So Luther speaks of the need of education in order that young men and women may understand their faith. The tract proceeds: if every burgher now, through God's mercy, has been released from iniquitous payments for indulgences, masses, monks, pilgrimages and the like, let him give part of this for schools, where boys now may learn more in three years than as heretofore in forty, when they became asses and blocks in the cloisters. Never before has Germany heard God's word as it is now heard. Let us then seize upon that word, lest it leave us as it left the Jews. There is no greater sin against God than not to teach the children. Do you say that this is the business of parents, not of town councils? But what if the parents do not do it: shall it then be neglected, and the authorities not have to answer? Often the parents are unfit, or have no time; and there are orphans. What is to become of city government if children are not educated? The business of a town is not merely to lay up wealth, but to bring up its citizens properly.

But someone says, why learn Latin, Greek and Hebrew, when we can have the Scriptures in German? So we Germans will ever be beasts, as other people call us. We would have foreign wares, and yet despise the foreign tongues and learning which might ennoble us! This is to continue German fools and beasts! We should accept the gift which God has given us, not without a purpose. He put his Scriptures in Hebrew and Greek: they are holy tongues. "Let us not think to hold the Gospel unless we hold the tongues." And, besides losing the Gospel from ignorance of the tongues, we should become unable to write Latin or German properly. A dreadful example is afforded by those schools and cloisters where they not only have mislearned the Gospel, but have fallen into a rotten Latin and German, like beasts. After apostolic times, as Greek and Hebrew disappeared, the Gospel, the Faith, Christendom, all declined, till they sank beneath a pope. Now the resurrection of the tongues has brought such light, that the world wonders at the purity of our gospel knowledge.

Here Luther points out that even Augustine erred in the interpretation of the Scripture through ignorance of the tongues; while that greatest of teachers, St. Bernard, is often carried beyond the true meaning. From lack of the tongues, the good Fathers encumbered the text with comment quite beside the point. "For as the sun is to the shadow, so is the tongue to all the Fathers' glosses." They would have been happy if only they could have learned as we can.

Luther proceeds further: though there were neither soul, nor heaven, nor hell, the government requires the education of boys and girls, in order that excellent and capable men may govern the land, and the women may manage their households. By pleasant methods children should be taught the tongues and liberal arts, with history, mathematics and music. "I only wish I had read more history and poetry myself." In fine, educated people are needed for worldly as well as spiritual functions. There should be libraries for books, from which we may well omit the Commentaries of the Jurists on the Law and of the theologians on the Sentences, as well as *Quaestiones* and monks' sermons. Have the Holy Scriptures first of all, in Latin, Greek, Hebrew and German, and if need be, other languages; with the best interpreters. The libraries should also contain books which aid linguistic studies; and the poets and orators, heathen and Christian,

Greek and Latin. One learns grammar from them. Also text-books of the liberal arts, of law and medicine; with chronicles and histories, which preserve good tales.

It behoved Luther to urge the reinstatement of education. For the Lutheran revolt, reformation, awakening, however one may call it, troubled the universities, which needed troubling then as always, to keep their waters fresh; it also distracted the attention of students from their humane studies, and drew their spirits into the maelstrom of religious disturbance and revival, to the temporary dislocation of all other intellectual interests. Erasmus was not alone in saying, "Wherever Lutheranism reigns, there is an end to letters. Yet these men have been nourished and helped by letters."

Luther's revolt from papal authority and his reformed faith did not spring from humanism and arise in humanistic circles as clearly, or to the same degree, as the Reform in France. Nevertheless Erfurt with its university, where Luther received much of his education, was humane and liberal; and there he associated with as ardent humanists as Germany afforded. He was moderately read in the classics; but such classical allusions as may be found through his writings seem largely taken from the *Adagia* of Erasmus. Yet even in France, the Reformed religion, as it became more sternly conscious of its principles and aims, drew apart from humanism, naturally, since humanism in the main was pagan, or at least of this world, and the Reform was bent on Christian salvation. Likewise, Luther, with the impulses, energies, purposes of his dominantly religious nature set upon the proof and vindication of his faith, could not possibly be interested in classical studies for their own sake. Nor was he a man that was likely to maintain intimate and trusted relations with those whose aims and interests were quite different from his own. On their side, the humanists discovered that Luther's ways and Luther's interests were not theirs. They were free-minded men and patriotic Germans, who disliked the papal church as unfriendly to liberal studies and oppressive to Germany. The most typical production of these humanists was the book of *Letters of Obscure Men,* indicted in the Reuchlin controversy, a controversy which was altogether theirs.[42]

But Germans who were devoted to liberal studies were not alike in other respects, nor moved by the same motives. Beyond this common taste, there was little likeness between Ulrich von Hutten and Mutianus. When Luther had posted his Theses, and afterwards defied Rome both as a German and a true believing and enlightened Christian, his cause attracted the sympathies of humane scholars and roused the truculent enthusiasm of such a one as Hutten. Hutten lived long enough to quarrel with Erasmus, but his violent anti-papal soul found no reason to draw back from Luther, and would rather have urged the Wittenberger on to bloodier war against the Roman tyrant. Other humane scholars, Melanchthon, chief among them, merged themselves enthusiastically in the Lutheran movement, or kept manfully by its side. But quite as many, caring for letters above all things, and fearing to imperil their temporal fortunes and eternal souls in warfare with the Church, drew back from the Reformer, choosing to remain in the bosom of the mother who had nourished their souls, and might either clothe or castigate their tender bodies.

The body of Erasmus was extremely tender, and its wants insistent. Nor was he inclined toward strenuous defense of any cause save that of liberal thought and study. Our observation of him in a previous chapter has disclosed how impossible it was for an Erasmus to march hand in hand with Luther. The parting of their ways typified the incompatibility between devotion to letters and absorption in an enthusiastic evangelical agitation. It remains to see what Luther thought of Erasmus.

Early in March, 1517, Luther writes: "I am reading our Erasmus, and day by day my estimation of him lessens.

42 Above, Chap. 1.

It pleases me how learnedly he convicts monks and priests of their inveterate and sleepy ignorance;[43] but I fear that he does not sufficiently emphasize Christ and God's grace wherein he is much more ignorant than Lefèvre of Étaples.[44] Human considerations outweigh the divine with him." [45] Thus from the first, Luther discerned rational ethics rather than religious unction in Erasmus's attitude toward religion and Scripture.

In September 1521, Luther will not listen to a suggestion coming from Erasmus that he should show himself more moderate. "His opinion has not the slightest weight with me. . . . when I see him far from a knowledge of grace, and in all his writings looking to peace rather than to the cross of Christ. He thinks all these matters should be handled politely and gently; but Behemoth cares not for that, nor will emendment come of it. I remember, in his preface to the New Testament, that he says, referring to himself, that Christian easily despises glory. But, O Erasmus, I fear, you err. Magna res est gloriam contemnere!" [46]

So he closes with a pious but quite human gibe. Three years later when Luther's friends no longer spared Erasmus, and that gifted man was also dipping his pen in gall, Luther wrote directly to him, asking that there might be at least a friendly truce between them.[47] Later, however, for the benefit of his son John, he characterized Erasmus as the "enemy of all religions and especially hostile to that of Christ, a perfect exemplar and type of Epicurus and Lucian." [48] Finally in 1534 Luther wrote to his friend Amsdorff, lengthily criticising the man Erasmus, his pernicious views of religion, and his erroneous understand-

---

[43] Seems to refer to reliance on ritual, etc.

[44] See Vol. III, Chap. 8, n. 1.

[45] De Wette, I, p. 52.

[46] De Wette, II, p. 49-50.

[47] De Wette, II, p. 498; April, 1524. Erasmus was already writing his *De libero arbitrio* against Luther.

[48] De Wette, IV, 497.

ing of Scripture. The letter leaves very little of him un-condemned, and ends with the wish that his works might be excluded from the schools, since even when harmless they are useless.[49]

Long before this, these two protagonists, the one of religion the other of humane piety, sacred and profane, had crossed arguments on the weighty matter of human free will and God's fore-ordainment. Erasmus, fretted by the stress of many subtle as well as palpable compulsions to declare against Luther, could refrain no longer. Had he selected purgatory, pilgrimages or indulgences, as the topic of his polemic, his argument must have stultified his real agreement with Luther upon such matters. But as a humanist in the broadest sense, he could not but uphold human liberty and the freedom of the will. This topic fell in with the scope and temper of his intellectual life; and as a subject of philosophy suited his position in the eyes of men. He treated it rationally and humanly, as a subject of discussion and opinion, yet adduced the support of scriptural passages.

The topic was vital to Luther's conception of God and man and the nexus of creatorship and creaturehood between them. For years he had devoted study and earnest consideration to it, and as early as 1516 had composed in scholastic fashion a searching *Quaestio de viribus et voluntate hominis sine gratia*.[50] With him it was a question of Christian faith, of salvation or damnation. Naturally, in 1525, as he wrote his *de servo arbitrio* in confutation of Erasmus's *de libero arbitrio*, he condemned his opponent's attitude in treating the subject as a matter of phil-

---

[49] De Wette, IV, pp. 507-520. Cf. another letter to Amsdorff, De Wette, IV, p. 545. There is a good deal in Luther's *Table Talk* on Erasmus's foolishness as a theologian, and his utter failure to recognize the function and meaning of Christ. See e.g. Preger, *Tischreden Luthers* (Leipzig 1888) nos. 357, 365.

[50] ("Inquiry concerning the strength and will of the man without grace.") Stange, *Quellenschriften zur Ges. des Protestantismus* I. (Leipzig 1904).

osophical opinion and probability. "The Holy Ghost is no sceptic, and has not written dubious opinions in our hearts, but solid certitudes,—more solid and assured than life and all experiences."

You say, Erasmus, continues Luther warming to his argument, that all things in Scripture are not necessary for faith, and that some matters in it are obscure, and you cite Romans XI, 33, "O the depth of the riches both of the wisdom and knowledge of God! how unsearchable are his judgments, and his ways past tracing out." But I say: "God and God's scripture are two things; just as the Creator and the creation are two things. No one doubts that much is hidden in God that we do not know. . . . But that anything in Scripture is confused and not plain and clear, is a notion spread abroad by the godless sophists, with whose mouth thou speakest, Erasmus; but they have never brought forward an article, nor can they, through which this madness of theirs could be established."

To be sure, continues Luther, to one ignorant of the language and grammar of Scripture, much may be hidden; but not because of the height or difficulty of the substance. All is written for our instruction, and any seeming obscurity is due to the blindness of the reader. It is not to be endured that you put this matter of free will among those which are needless. On the contrary, we must know what the will can do and how it stands in relation to God's grace. We must distinguish surely between what is God's work and what is ours, if we would be righteous. "It is also necessary and salutary for Christians to know that God foreknows nothing casually and conditionally; but that He foreknows, preordains and accomplishes all through His unchanging and eternal and unfailing will. This principle like a lightning stroke, strikes to earth and crushes out free will."

After some folios of Christian argument, these sentences are amplified as follows in Luther's final conclusions:

"For if we believe that God foreknows and foreordains all things, and in his foreknowledge and fore-ordainment can neither be deceived nor hindered, then nothing can take place that He does not Himself will. Reason must admit this, while itself bears witness that there is no free will in men or angels or in any creature. So if we believe Satan to be the Prince of the World, who fights against the Kingdom of God in order that bounden men may not be loosed, and that he is overcome through the divine strength of the Spirit, it is again clear that there can be no free will. Likewise, if we believe that original sin has vitiated us . . . there is nothing left that can turn to good, but only to evil. . . . In fine, if we believe that Christ has saved men through his blood, we must acknowledge that the whole man was lost; otherwise we shall make Christ unnecessary, or into a Saviour of the most worthless part. This were blasphemous and sacrilegious."

The modern man is loosed quite otherwise from this particular predestination controversy,—or perhaps drawn to it by other chains. Luther's whole soul and faith were in it, and to his comfort. As he says substantially in his *Table Talk:* "when I think of the ineffable benefits God has prepared for me in Christ, then predestination becomes full of comfort: remove Christ, and all is shattered." The whole temperament of Luther is speaking and the sum of his convictions: the evangelical religious temperament, and the faith which it included.

Luther's faith was justified by its prodigious doctrinal effectiveness. His adamantine conservatism made his doctrines solid and tangible as rocks; they had body; they could be grasped and held to; and they had the sanction of divine authority. They were not presented as novelties, but were restored to men. Luther gave men what they had already, or might have had at any time from Scripture. And the doctrine which he had to offer, the Pauline Christian Gospel, was in itself so good, so comforting and assuring, so saving in this present troubled life, as well as for that to come.

Thus not only from logical necessity, but actually, Luther's clinging religious and social conservatism was an integral element of his reforms. These present a course of enforced surrender and substitution: the enforced surrender of one intolerable belief after another, and the substitution of the Scriptural doctrine or principle as he understood it. He kept what he could of the religion in which he had been reared, adhering to every belief, practice, or function of the contemporary Roman Catholic Church that the progress of his Scriptural faith and the logic and exigencies of his polemic state permitted him to retain.

His primal sources of strength and confidence lay in his mighty appropriation of the Pauline doctrine of justification by faith. It became the main criterion of his retentions and rejections. Another pillar of his strength was his conception of a Church universal, in which the papacy was but an incident and an evil one. He threw aside the hierarchical papal monarchy [51] for the older Pauline and Augustinian conception of a communion of true believers. Thus, with certain differences, Wyclif had done before him; and so should Calvin and other succeeding reformers do.[52]

[51] Cf. Harnack, *Dogmengeschichte*, III, pp. 410 sqq. Third edition.

[52] Luther gives his conception in the third part of his elaborate tract *upon Councils and Churches* written in 1539. He says that the Church according to the Creed is "a communion of the saints, a company or assembly of such people as are Christians and holy; that is, a Christian, holy, company or church. . . . The holy Christian Church is holy Christendom or the entire Christendom. In the Old Testament it is called the people of God." It is a pity, says he, that we have not kept that unequivocal expression "the holy Christian people of God"; for that is what the Church is. This Church, this holy Christian people of God, it recognized by the following works: It possesses God's Word; uses the sacraments of baptism and the Communion. It holds the *Keys* and uses them openly so that when a Christian sins, he shall be punished, and if not bettered, shall be cast out, bound in his sins. It selects and calls its servants, to wit, its bishops, pastors, preachers, who ad-

Justification by faith, a universal church of believers, the freedom of the Christian man, not in his own will but God's: here was enough to stay a strong brave man against the papal dragon. Luther purged religion, even made those purge it who hated him. Yet one queries whether his teaching held as much of Christianity as did that great age-long institution of the Roman Catholic Church. It would have been hard for one man to be as universal as the Roman Catholic Church, which was built upon man as well as upon God. Lutheranism has changed and subdivided. And the Catholic Church in spite of its monarch pope, its vain absolutions, its excommunications and its interdicts, lives on. In spite of its mammon of abuses and corruption? Rather, because of it! For the Roman Catholic Church rests upon the imperfections and corruptions, as well as on the common needs, of man. It still has many saints; yet neither now, nor in Luther's time or before him, does its Catholicism point to truth for truth's sake, or to righteousness for the sake of righteousness. Its soul looks to the loaves and fishes, if not of this world, then of Heaven. Never could the Roman Church be supplanted by that mighty swashbuckler of the spirit, Martin Luther, though he was himself as much and

---

minister its holy things or offices, named above. God's people are also recognized by their public prayer and singing of psalms and spiritual songs; and by their holy cross of (a) enduring the persecution of the world, the flesh, and the devil, and (b) obeying the authorities. Such are the constituents of Christian holiness; and there are besides the outer signs of good conduct in all things according to the Commandments of God. The devil has aped God's holy Church in the papacy and its institutions and ceremonies through which papists think they will be saved. Yet beware, on the other hand, of those who cry Spirit! spirit! and decry all outer observances.

In closing, he says that the school is needed to educate true preachers; next, the household to provide scholars, then the Rathaus to protect the citizens. The Church, God's own house and city, draws its protection from the city, and its members from the household. So the three orders are household, city, Church.

as many things as a man could be; everything from a foul-mouthed German peasant to the mightiest of religious seers, and withal the greatest German we have known.

Appendix to Chapter 4

MELANCHTHON AND ZWINGLI

THERE WERE TWO MEN very different from each other in their characters and careers, who when they met, met as partial opponents, and were not permitted to agree by the masterful Luther who held them apart: Melanchthon and Zwingli. With respect to their inclinations and functions they may also be regarded as people working at some half way station between Luther and Erasmus, a position more apparent with Melanchthon than with the vigorous and independent Swiss reformer.

In the Lutheran movement Melanchthon is second only to his chief in importance and effect; his is the one name besides Luther's which has survived in popular fame. There was reverence and affection between the two, which continued unbroken to the end, though sometimes strained. Melanchthon worked under Luther's leadership though not altogether under his dominance; and Luther held him to be far more gifted than himself. The tutelary deity of Melanchthon's youth was Reuchlin, his great-uncle, who saw to his university education and advancement and in 1518 obtained a call for him from the Elector to teach Greek at Wittenberg, when Melanchthon was only twenty-one years old. He was indeed a youthful prodigy in his studies and intellectual development; nor did his faculties weaken with the advance of years and knowledge. His attainments drew the admiration of Erasmus, with whom he remained on good terms; for he was a man inclined to stay at peace with all. Humanist, scholar, educator, promoter of the classical languages and thought, Melanchthon would gladly have devoted himself to Greek, and might have preferred it to theology. But as he clove at once to Luther, his labors, like his destinies, were cast in the fields of the great conflict.

Next to Luther himself, Melanchthon became par excellence the champion, the expounder, and the formulator of Lutheranism. He defended his chief in an Apology directed against the "Furious decree of the Paris Theologasters," the Sorbonne to wit, who had declared Luther an arch-heretic. Like his leader, he wrote against the murderous peasants, and after the deed, he approved the burning of Servetus in Geneva. He was, however, more conciliatory, and given to dreams of peace where Luther saw there could be none, as at the Augsburg diet. The Augsburg Confession and Apology were his masterpieces of Protestant formulation.

His chief work of theological exposition was of course the *Loci Communes theologici,* which emerging from an embryonic *Adumbratio,* proceeded onward through a first and second and third *Aetas* to its final bulk and form. Even as Calvin's *Institute.* And it is a matter of no slight interest to note that as Melanchthon's work and Calvin's reached their final form, they followed more closely the arrangement of the Lombard's *Sentences* and the *Summa* of Aquinas. The fact was that for the Lombard and Aquinas, as for Augustine before them, and later for Calvin and Melanchthon, Scripture itself furnished the arrangement of a work that should comprehend Scriptural doctrine. Says Melanchthon at the beginning of his *Secunda Aetas:* "Habet ipsa scriptura suam quandam methodum et quidem artificiosam. Series enim dogmatum ab ipso ordine historiae aptissime sumi potest. Initio de creatione, de peccato hominis, de promissionibus loquitur, postea tradit legem, deinde docit Evangelium de Christo: —" [1] most aptly we arrange our matter after the order

---

[1] ("Even the Scripture displays its own method and technique. Indeed the sequence of the dogma can be best followed from the very beginning of history. The Scripture starts with Creation, then proceeds to the Original Sin, thence to the Prophets, and finally to passing down the Law and the Gospel of Christ:—")

of Scriptural history; creation, man's sin, the promises, the law, and finally the Gospel.[2]

In this excellent work Melanchthon draws away from *scholasticae nugae;* and likewise from the *Aristotelicae argutiae,* although philosophically he held a profound respect for the Stagirite, and deemed his system salutary as a barrier against the *philosophical* disorder of the age. But the statements and arguments of the *Loci Communes* in the main are based on Scripture, and much more directly than those for instance of the *Summa* of Aquinas. For unlike the *Summa,* the *Loci Communes* does not move and find its substance in Aristotelian categories of thought. Melanchthon rather intended it as an ordered *Summa* of the Scriptural *Testimonia.* The new learning is present throughout the smooth Latin exposition of this master of clarity; and the work is humanistically flavored with Greek words and classical allusions. For the author was first and last a scholar, loving classical scholarship for its own sake. He also liked to find the analogues to scriptural truth in the lives and precepts of pagan philosophers; as one sees so clearly in those paragraphs where he arranges the precepts of the Law of Nature in correspondence with the Decalogue.[3] His liberal humanistic inclinations drew him toward Erasmus's side instead of Luther's in the controversy upon the freedom of the human will, which is evident in the *Secunda Aetas* of his *Loci* of 1535 and becomes even more pronounced in the corresponding sections of the *Tertia Aetas* of 1543.[4]

Confidence in the best in classical literature and philosophy, respect for the *lumen naturale* which the Fall of man darkened, but did not destroy, and recognition of the

[2] Melanchthon's *Loci Communes* occupy Vols. XXI and XXII of the *Corpus Reformatorum,* where the work is printed in its three stages, of 1521, 1535 and 1543. The passage quoted is from col. 254 of Vol. XXI; compare with it col. 341 of the same volume.

[3] *Loci Com. De lege naturae.* Third *Aetus* Vol. XXI, *Corp. Ref.* Col. 711 sqq.

[4] Vol. XXI, *Corp. Ref.* Col. 274 sqq. and col. 652 sqq.

lex naturae, worked together to strengthen the moral quality of Melanchthon's theology, and broadened its consideration of natural reason and the conscience of mankind. All this tended to moralize his theology, as his tempered exclusion of Aristotelian arguments tended to simplify it. Again, it was his natural reason and moral conscience that insisted on the freedom of the human will, and afforded an independent testimony in favor of the soul's immortality.

Melanchthon was a moral theologian, and a moral philosopher, and in all his labors for education never lost sight of the moral betterment which should result from learning. He strove so to enlarge and complete the plan of education that it might embrace all revealed or tested truth. To that end he was wont to use the pagan elements to fill out the Christian scheme. His study of antiquity was Catholic. He admired Plato, yet followed Aristotle; and as was natural for a sixteenth century humanist, he found moral and philosophic discussions adapted to his taste and comprehension in the works of the eclectic Cicero. Following Aristotle, imbibing Cicero, he produced manuals of Dialectic, Physics, Ethics, or edited the Aristotelian treatises on these topics; and composed Greek and Latin grammars, and other books for the schools. This great array of admirable text books, which carried far and wide his stimulating personal instructions, earned for him the honored title of *Praeceptor Germaniae,* which more than one educational worthy had borne before him.

Zwingli was never a follower of Luther, but rather an opponent, though holding some of the same doctrines. He was bred to an utterly different social and political régime; his convictions did not come from Wittenberg, although their development appears to have been influenced by Luther's writings. The two men were of independent and rather opposite temperaments, and, when they met, parted in confirmed disagreement. Zwingli is supposed to have been jealous of Luther's power, and

Luther always disapproved both of Zwingli and his views, and thought at last that his fate rightly came on him in the battle of Kappel; for, having taken the sword, he perished by it; and if God received him into blessedness He did it *extra regulam!* [5]—which is to say, acting not strictly in accord with Luther's ideas.

Zwingli was born in 1484 in the Toggenburg valley, dominion over which was disputed by Zurich and Schwyz. In 1518 he was elected priest and preacher for the great Zurich Minister; and thenceforth guided that city's political as well as religious destinies, in a way that anticipated the career of Calvin at Geneva. For Zwingli was a Swiss civic personality and politician before he became a reformer. From a certain teacher at Basel named Wyttenbach, he early took the principle of justification by faith, learned to look to Scripture as the Christian authority, and also to disapprove of papal indulgences. His education was mainly humanistic, and drawn from various masters. He professed to admire and follow Erasmus. But he was taken by the writings of Pico della Mirandula; and he drew from the Classics much that entered his life and affected the development of his convictions. He was a Greek scholar, and a student of the New Testament, who preferred the text to the commentators. He was also a reader of the Church Fathers. The Church was less powerful in Switzerland than in other countries, less well organized and correspondingly infected with looseness of conduct. But the papacy was tenderly disposed toward the people of the little mountain land, where its pay drew unequalled soldiers, of which the present papal guard is the last survival. Although he had profited from it, Zwingli declared himself opposed to this mercenary service and to the papal pensions which corrupted Swiss politics and people. He was rather anti-papal from the beginning; and readily yielded to his developing protestantism to disavow the pope's authority. He was a

5 Preger, *Luthers Tischreden,* no. 218, cf. no. 509.

preacher and a priest; yet his life was rather loose, and in 1524 he married.

By this time a general change in the forms of worship had been effected at Zurich, Zwingli leading the movement. The church there was made civic and democratic; its offices were reformed and translated into German; images were discarded, and the Mass abolished (April, 1525); the monasteries were secularized, and their incomes devoted to charity or education. A struggle followed with the Anabaptists, who were for the most part expelled. The further course of Zwingli's life was involved in a tangle of politics, connected with the progress or blocking of the Reform in Switzerland.

Zwingli's formulation of a Christian faith was not as important as Luther's on the one hand, or as Calvin's on the other. If it was not carried through with the originative religious power of the one, or the insistent logic of the other, it was reasonable and genial. Politician, man of action, as he was, Zwingli was also a reader and a student. And, as is common with able busy men, who are also great readers, he assembled thoughts from many quarters, worked them into his convictions or philosophy, but had neither the slow meditative leisure nor the inner power to transform the matter of his reading into a seamless system. Yet he grasped with energy the Pauline Augustinian justification through faith, and genially and humanely enlarged his religious conceptions with thoughts drawn from Seneca's eclectic but predominantly Stoic store, or from the undigested mass of borrowed and yet temperamentalized ideas offered by the works of Pico. Through them, and independently of them, he gleaned from many minds thoughts which served his working faith. Withal, and this is a vital point, inasmuch as he was a man of action, a man of working faith, and a reformer of religious practice and doctrine, he did not fail to vitalize his teachings and endue them with qualities of power, by which men might live and endure, or fight.

With Seneca, philosophy was a way to virtue. It was

a religion with him; and it became an integral part of the religion of Zwingli. Seneca expressed as much trust in God as was felt by a Paul or an Augustine. He had also said: "We are born in a kingdom; liberty is to obey God." God has the qualities of a Father, and is also the *summum bonum* for all. Zwingli adds the thought that believers are his willing instruments, working along with him for their only good, and for the glory which is in the fulfilment of the divine purpose: a mighty thought.

Zwingli advanced still further in his eclectic stoicism and Augustinianism, following his own impulse too, and found God to be the sum total of good, that is of being: "unum ac solum infinitum . . . praeter hoc nihil esse." Universal being, (esse rerum universarum) is the being of God, (esse numinis).[6] Hence God includes all finite beings, who are part of Him and his universal plan. He is the founder, ruler, administrator of the universe. Man alone shall not stand without the scope of God's all-determining purpose. Zwingli brings the full stoical conception of *providence* into the Christian scheme of election.[7]

God reveals himself in the consciousness and consciences of men; and creates faith within them. That faith is true which directs itself solely to God; superstition consists in reliance upon other things.[8] He revealed himself to the minds of the chosen heathen, as well as to the flock of Christ. So with Zwingli, the outer revelation ceased to be all important; and incidents and observances became of no importance. He was disposed to discard the special miracle and intervention: why demand the particular supernatural manifestation when God is the sole first cause, and works all things in all, to the exclusion of secondary causes. Surely he who finds God working everywhere will need no special miracles. So Zwingli would admit no miracle in the

6 For these citations and more besides, I am indebted to Dilthey, *Auffassung etc des Menschen im 15. und 16. Jahrhundert.*

7 In Zwingli's *De providentia.*

8 Zwingli, *De vera et falsa religione.*

Eucharist, no miraculous real presence such as Luther held to. For him, the sacrament was a memorial and a sign.

The outer ceremony may be negligible, indifferent. But there is a highest visible manifestation of the will and law of God, which men may bring to pass, working in faith: it is the Christian community or State, founded on the observance of God's law as well as on the promise of His Gospel. Here was again the mighty thought with which Calvin should build, Knox preach, and Cromwell smite, all of them willing instruments of God. No Lutheran church formed under the protection of an autocratic prince, and obediently adapting at least its outer self to the existent institutions and policy of a secular state, could even entertain such an ideal.